Selkie Summer

Margaret McAllister

Illustrated by **Daniela Terrazzini**
and **Darling Clementine**

OXFORD
UNIVERSITY PRESS

Letter from the Author

There were all sorts of influences on *Selkie Summer*, most of them to do with long-ago holidays in Scotland. I've included lovely clean beaches, appalling weather and quirky little holiday cottages.

The most important memory though is of a holiday in Scotland – but not on an island – when I was just about to start high school. I made friends with a curly-haired girl called Claire. We have been best friends since that first day, and are godmothers to each other's children!

Also in here is my love of Scottish history and folklore. Historians are finding out more and more about the past, but there's still a lot that we can only guess at. By the end of this story, you may know more of the island's secrets than Lily and Jess do.

Margaret McAllister

Chapter 1
The Last Summer

Lily's Diary

This morning I knew that ENOUGH WAS ENOUGH. I am so sick and tired of perching on the edge of a trench brushing bits of stone. I don't care if they dig up an entire skeleton, or hundreds of them. I don't care if there's a queen in there. I don't care if they've been buried upside down with their heads in porridge pots. I DON'T CARE!

I had to get out. So I did.

This is how it had all started.

Lily's parents had first met when they were digging up a battlefield, and they'd been digging things up ever since. They both taught history and archaeology at universities and were always going away on digs – visiting places where historical secrets might be hidden in the earth, making trenches and examining what they found. Lily's dad was very tall, with twinkly eyes and a bushy beard. If not for his dancing eyes, he might have looked unapproachable. Her mum was one of those people who always looked elegant, even when she was working on a dig, dirty and wearing old clothes and trying to keep her hair out of her eyes.

Lily had been accompanying her parents on digs for as long as she could remember. If a dig was happening in the school holidays and other archaeologists took their families with them, the kids would all get together. Digs like that had been fun. But not this one!

This one was on a remote Scottish island. They were excavating a site that might be concealing secrets, or might not. It could be a thousand-year-old monastery, or (as Lily's father said cheerfully) the monastery graveyard, in which case they could find out about how the monks had died. ('Boredom,' said Lily, but nobody was listening.) There could even be a Viking settlement hidden down there. (*Oh, like all the other Viking settlements you've dug up over the last ten years,* thought Lily.) Or they might not find anything much. Who knew, until they'd excavated?

For most of her life Lily had accepted it was inevitable she'd spend her holidays on the edge of a muddy field, but this year was different. She had explained that this year she wanted to go on a summer holiday without digging *anything* up, especially a thousand-year-old man who'd died from some disgusting disease. She'd rather have stayed with Granny, but Granny would be away all summer. Because the most important thing – the thing that Mum and Dad just couldn't understand – was that this was The Last Summer. She'd just had her twelfth birthday. In August, she'd start at Cameron Road High School.

Most of her friends would be going to Cameron Road too, but not all of them. It was such a big step – one that would change everything! Didn't her parents remember when they started high school? She'd be leaving a school where nobody was more than twelve, and moving to one where the oldest students could drive cars and vote in elections. And no going back.

'It'll be fine.' That was what everyone said. Maybe it would, but Lily had been anticipating one last wild, silly summer with her primary school friends before everything changed for ever. One last summer when they could all push each other on the swings, trampoline in back gardens and play tennis badly in the park – that was all she wanted. She wanted to be in Edinburgh because Edinburgh was home and she loved it.

Sadly, Mum and Dad didn't get it. They just kept telling her how much she'd love the island when she got there – but Lily had heard this too many times to believe it. They even said it in the relentless rain on the way to this horrible cold, wet rock. From the air, the island lay alone in the grey sea as if the mainland didn't like it and had kicked it out.

'It'll be fine when we get there!' Mum said when Lily threw up on the aeroplane that looked as if it had come from a toyshop.

'It'll be fine!' they said when they landed in a sweep of wind and rain that nearly flung Lily off her feet.

'You'll love the cottage!' they called as they staggered uphill dragging suitcases over the rough, stony scree.

At that moment she didn't care what the cottage was like, so long as it had four walls and a roof. In fact, it was single storey and whitewashed, near the sea and extremely cosy, with a log fire awaiting them and low ceilings with wooden beams – but by the time they got there she was too drenched and exhausted to notice much. Dad kept banging his head on the beams (which was quite funny, but made him grumpy, which didn't help anyone). In Lily's room everything was in the same shade of blue grey, which reminded her unpleasantly of the sea. *Boring,* she thought.

'It'll be better when we meet the rest of the team,' said Mum.

They met them the next day at the dig site, on top of a windy hill. Most of them had arrived earlier by ferry, some of them with cars, and were staying in guest houses on the island. The first thing Lily found out was that none of them had brought families. She was the one and only person there under the age of twenty. Digging on the first trench had started and a few cabins and a block of portable toilets had been set up near it. They looked like grey boxes that had been put down for a moment and forgotten about. A second, smaller trench was further up the hill.

Apparently there was a local saying: 'If you can't see the next island, it's raining. If you *can* see it, it's about to rain.' For some reason that she couldn't understand, everyone found this very funny. There was a constant drizzle that was called 'Scotch mist' but felt like rain to Lily, and the sky hid in grey clouds as if it were sulking. The other archaeologists mostly ignored her. Lily didn't really mind, as she'd rather be ignored than condescended to like a five-year-old, but she was lonely. There was a small town at one end of the island, but it was at least two hours' walk. At the end of the first long, chilly day, all they had found was a broken clay pipe in one trench and a halfpenny in the other. The following day some pottery had turned up and everyone got very excited until it turned out to be bits of a teapot from the 1980s.

By the middle of the first week, the clouds were starting to disappear. Halfway through the morning Lily looked up to see a shimmer of pale blue in the sky, and soon it was warm enough to take off her waxed jacket. For the first time since coming here she felt the stirrings of happiness, and she wasn't going to waste it on a trench. She stood up and dusted soil from her jeans.

'I'm off for a walk on the beach, Mum,' she said.

Mum looked up, put down her trowel and pushed her hair out of her eyes.

'You don't know your way around,' she told Lily. 'The cliffs are steep and the weather here changes with no warning at all. Let's go for a long walk tomorrow, all together.'

'No!' It came out louder and angrier than Lily had meant it to.

Other people around them stopped talking and one of them dropped a trowel, which clattered much too loudly into a steel bucket. Lily sat down on the edge of the trench to speak to Mum quietly.

'Mum, I just really, really want to be on my own,' she begged. 'I've got my phone. I'll stay where I can see the cottage, OK?'

Mum thought for a moment, then pushed her hand into her back pocket. 'Here's a key to the cottage,' she said. 'If it rains, run in there. We'll come back for a lunch break around one o'clock.'

Finally, with a last, 'Lily! Don't lose that key!' ('I won't, Mum!') Lily was able to turn her back on the dig and clamber down the hill, past the cottage and down on to the beach where the cliffs to one side sheltered her from the wind and the vast blue-green sea swished delicate waves on to the shore. The soft, pale sand filled her trainers, so she made her way to the firm, damp shoreline where tiny crabs scuttled busily about and pale green seaweed sprawled at her feet. She stretched out her arms to the sea, the rocks and the wide sky, and took a few steps forwards so that the incoming waves came almost – but not quite – to her toes.

Those waves were too good to resist. She ran to the rocks on the south side of the bay, sat down to pull off her trainers and socks, left them on a rock and hurried back to the water's edge. The waves that tickled her feet were cold enough to make her stretch and curl her toes, but not cold enough to make her shiver. Turning her back on the rocks, she walked along the shore, letting the waves trickle over her feet and enjoying the feel of cool, wet sand. There were spiral shells, damply gleaming stones and pebbles, and fragments of green glass washed smooth by the sea.

Something from behind cannoned into her so hard that she stumbled and barely stayed on her feet. The words 'look where you're going' were already forming in her mouth, but then she stopped.

A large black-and-white dog was looking up at her, its ears pricked up and its long hairy tail wagging furiously. Its eyes were bright and one of Lily's socks dangled from its mouth.

'Molly!' A curly-haired girl about Lily's age in jeans, sweater and wellies was leaping down the rocks towards them. When she reached them, the dog sat down obediently.

'Molly, you mutt!' said the girl. *'Give!'*

The dog dropped the sock and scampered backwards as if she expected the curly-haired girl to throw it for her. But the girl had a ball in her hand and with a call of 'Chase that!' she flung it across the beach. The dog raced after it.

'Sorry about that,' said the girl, with a soft island accent. 'Molly's usually a good dog, but she has a thing about socks.'

Molly pounced on the ball, shook it and ran back to them with sand on her nose. She dropped the ball and sneezed.

Lily laughed. So did the other girl. Suddenly the cold, grubby dig seemed a long way away and the whole day looked better.

11

Chapter 2
Learning to Flurple

By the time they had walked all the way along the shore throwing the ball for Molly ('She's a collie cross – she should have been a sheepdog but she hasn't the brains for it') they had learned a lot about each other. Jess was exactly two months older than Lily ('The twenty-second? My birthday's the twenty-second too!') so they were both due to start high school in August. Jess had two younger brothers and her parents had at least five different jobs between them – boatbuilding, sheep farming, teaching music, working in a preschool, painting and decorating, and whatever else came their way. Like most people on the island they were crofters too, using their little patch of land to grow food and keep a few chickens. Jess had lived all her life on the island. She was learning the violin and piano. (Lily was learning the flute.) It turned out that they liked the same books, the same music and the same films. Lily soon liked Jess enough to admit shyly that she liked writing and illustrating stories, and Jess said, 'Oh, do you do that too? So do I!'

'Is there much to do on the island?' asked Lily.

'Oh, there's always something going on,' said Jess. 'There's the animals to see to, and we've got choirs and a drama group and dancing and all that, and sports teams.

And it's easy to get to the mainland – that's where the cinema is. The Internet's a bit slow sometimes, but mostly it's OK. Everyone relies on it. And we've got the wee primary school, but the high school's on the mainland.'

Lily had guessed that it must be. She hadn't seen all the island yet, but she couldn't imagine it having a high school. There wouldn't be enough pupils.

'Will you have to fly there?' she asked.

'Ach no, everyone goes on the ferry,' said Jess. She threw the ball again and looked up. 'We can go up here and over the headland, then back down to the beach on the other side.'

The beach, she said, was known as Jackie's Bay, but nobody knew who Jackie was. There were two paths leading down to it – the shallow one Lily had used ('the Slidie') and, at the other end, the steeper and rockier 'Selkie's Stair'. The climb up to the top of Selkie's Stair was hard, but the view over the bay made Lily gasp with delight. They stepped on to soft, springy turf so thick with small pink flowers that she couldn't even tiptoe without stepping on them.

'This bit's called the Braid,' Jess told her.

'What are these flowers?' asked Lily.

'It's only sea thrift,' said Jess, sounding surprised. 'Have you not seen them before?'

'I've never been anywhere like this,' said Lily. 'And I haven't seen any of the island, apart from the cottage and the excavation site.'

'Have you ever seen a seal?' asked Jess. 'I mean, in the wild? If you're lucky, we might see some today.' She led the way down to another stretch of sand and rocks. 'This is the long shore. Let me just put Molly on the lead in case she startles anything. So, where are your mum and dad digging?'

Lily turned and pointed up the hill. 'It's called Unfell,' she said. 'They haven't found anything, though.'

'Unfell?' said Jess. 'Are they looking for the – ' She stopped because Lily had grabbed her arm.

'Look!' whispered Lily.

Two seals, shining wet, whiskered and as round as barrels, sprawled idly on the rocks and flapped their tails gently. They looked up contentedly with large dark eyes. Lily stared with delight.

'That's *amazing*!' she said.

'Don't get too close,' warned Jess. 'They're usually no bother, but they can get grumpy if they have young ones with them. Look out to sea – there's another one.'

Lily looked. A dark whiskery face looked up from the water until a sudden swelling wave rose and swamped it. It bobbed up again with a good-natured expression on its round face. Lily felt that if she waved to it, it would wave back. One of the seals on the rocks rolled over as if it wanted to watch the clouds.

'I never knew they were so big!' whispered Lily. She couldn't help whispering, partly because she didn't want to alarm them, but also because seeing them so close was rather magical.

'If they stood up straight, they'd be about as tall as us,' replied Jess.

'Stood up!' said Lily, and they both laughed at the idea of a big, blubbery seal standing on its tail and holding out its absurd little flippers.

'I thought they were meant to be graceful!' said Lily.

'They are when they're swimming,' Jess told her. 'That's where they're beautiful. They're fast and clever in the sea. On land they just sprawl, or, you know, kind of flurple about if they have to get anywhere.'

'Flurple?' repeated Lily.

Jess giggled. 'Yes, they kind of – well, they just flurple. There isn't a proper word for it. Here, I'll show you. Lie on your tum like this.'

Jess demonstrated and Lily copied her.

'Keep your feet together,' said Jess. 'Now hold your elbows tucked right into your sides. Now try to move. See if you can get to that patch of daisies.'

Lily tried, but with her feet together and her elbows tucked in, nothing seemed to move much. She managed a kind of caterpillar crawl and rolled over and over laughing.

'They do it like this!' called Jess, and did something between a crawl and a rock. 'Watch, this is flur – ' She couldn't finish for laughing, and they had breathless, giggly flurpling races until Lily saw that it was one o'clock and she should be back. She dusted herself down.

'That's where we're staying,' she said, pointing. 'I should be able to get away again this afternoon, if Mum and Dad don't need me to help with anything.'

'Me too,' said Jess. 'I could call for you if you like. What time?' She slid a hand into her pocket and took out a mobile phone.

'We'll swap numbers too, but sometimes you can get a signal and sometimes you can't,' she explained. 'It depends on what network you're on, and whereabouts on the island you are, and sometimes you just have to stand on top of a hill and point it in the right direction. What's your number?'

They exchanged numbers and Lily ran all the way back to the cottage. Jess, Molly and the seals had given her energy. She wanted to tell everyone about how well the morning had turned out, and all about her new friend, and the seals and sea thrift.

Jess's diary

I have a new friend! YES!!

Her name's Lily and we have so much in common it's amazing. She starts high school next year too, but hers will be in Edinburgh just a few streets from where she lives – lucky her! She's not been on the island long but it's been dry today, so she's had a chance to see it. In the morning we walked the shore and saw some seals, then this afternoon we went all over the place.

On McLeod's Hill we saw a wee red squirrel in a tree, and then there was a stag in the valley and Lily loved all that.

Lily's here with her parents, who are doing a dig at Unfell. Wonder if they'll let me go and join in? I'd love to. I wonder if they're looking for the Viking princess.

I might tell Lily about high school and everything, but not yet. It's different for her. Maybe when I know her better.

The forecast was for a storm and the wind's rising now. It's going to be a wild night!

Chapter 3
Selkies and Vikings

That night, Lily went to bed feeling that the island was exactly the right place to be. Her bedroom, with its blue-grey painted walls, wasn't boring any more. It was as if the sea were all around her, except that ...

There is no such colour as sea blue, or sea green, she wrote in her diary, sitting up in bed. *The sea changes colour all the time. It can even be more than one colour at the same time. Sometimes it's even turquoise.*

She closed the diary, put out the light and lay listening. All evening the wind had been rising and now it raged round the cottage as if it were throwing a tantrum. Flurries of rain battered the window.

On the day they arrived on the island she had hated the wind and rain – but then she had been outside, cross and airsick. Now, with a good day behind her, she was snuggled into a warm bed. The storm could do what it liked. It couldn't touch her. That felt good.

* * *

In the morning the storm was still sweeping across the island. Dad had abandoned his muddy boots outside the front door the night before and now they were nowhere to be seen. (One of them turned up later snared in a bush and the other was found on a chicken-shed roof.)

As long as the wild weather lasted, there was no chance of any serious digging. Mum, Dad and the rest of the team decided to spend the day trawling through the notes they'd already written, and writing yet more.

Lily tried to phone Jess but there was no signal in the cottage, so she put on her jacket and shoes and went outside where she had to turn her back to the wind and huddle in the doorway as she held up the phone and turned it round. She was still doing that when a muddy four-wheel drive drew up outside and Jess jumped out, pulling the hood of her jacket closely round her face. She shouted something, but the wind whipped the sound away.

'Come in the house!' yelled Lily and they ran indoors. She'd been outside for less than a minute but her jacket was soaked.

'Mum says,' gasped Jess, a bit out of breath, 'do you want to come to our house today?'

'Yes, please!' said Lily at the same time as Mum said, 'That's very kind!'

'And she says,' said Jess, looking at Lily's mum, 'the boat most likely won't be in today, so would you like to have a meal with us tonight?'

Mum stared at Jess and clearly didn't know what she was talking about. It was as if Jess had just started speaking in Gaelic.

'Sorry,' she said, 'the boat? I don't understand.'

'The boat should be coming in today with the supplies,' Jess explained patiently. 'All the things for the shops, and whatever people have ordered – only it won't get through in weather like this, and sometimes when the boat doesn't get through there isn't much left in the shop, especially when the island's busy. But Mum's got lots of stuff in the freezer and she says you're welcome to come and have tea with us.'

'Oh, I see!' answered Mum, and went on to say about how it was very kind, but they couldn't possibly be such a nuisance, and to please say thank you to Jess's mother.

Lily felt very embarrassed and hoped that Jess's parents wouldn't feel insulted. Besides, she would have loved to have tea at Jess's house.

'Ach well, Lily can stay and have lunch with us today anyway,' said Jess. 'Is that all right?'

To Lily's relief it was, and she hurried to pull on her wellies and run outside with Jess. The four-wheel drive smelled of damp dog, damp people and hay. Jess's mum, who was called Ellie Jameson, was a tall, cheerful, curly-haired woman who drove with the windscreen wipers swishing and squeaking and the music turned up.

Prickly yellow gorse bushes covered the hillsides and the road was so narrow that, if a car came the other way, one of the drivers had to reverse into a passing place to let the other one through.

At last, they stopped outside a whitewashed stone house rather like the one where Lily's family were staying but much bigger, with a vegetable plot and a few flowers growing near the door. The house looked patched together, as if parts of it had grown out of other parts or been added on at random. A shed had been built against one side and a garage on the other, and a glass porch at the front was full of wellies and geraniums.

A little way from the house was a barn with a corrugated iron roof. 'That's the lambing shed, but we don't use it this time of year,' explained Jess.

A chicken hopped down from a hut inside a wire netting run, pecked at the ground, ruffled its feathers crossly and scurried back inside as the car stopped.

'That's Missy,' said Jess. 'She's one of mine.'

'You have your own chickens?' said Lily.

'Yes, I have three,' said Jess. 'They're all laying just now. I can give you some eggs. Mum, will I take Molly for a quick run?'

'I don't suppose Lily wants to go out when it's blowing a hooly,' said Mrs Jameson. She was right – Lily didn't want to be outside for any longer than necessary – but she didn't want Jess to think she was a wimp. She pulled her hood up.

'It's fine – I don't mind!' she said, and suddenly she and Jess were running uphill with their backs to the wind, holding on to each other to stay upright, laughing and dragging wet hair back from their faces.

From here, they could look down at a rain-streaked huddle of houses, small shops, a primary school and a church.

'That's Ollerswick!' called Jess against the wind. 'That's the town!'

Molly ran uphill with her ears streaming back in the wind as she sniffed and followed trails until Jess shouted, 'Molly! *Fish*!' which made the dog whisk round and gallop home. For a moment, as they lurched into the porch, Lily caught a glimpse of herself in a mirror. Her stinging cheeks were pink, her hair wild and her eyes bright, and she felt wonderfully, breathlessly alive. Jess fussed over Molly, drying her and feeding her cold cooked fish.

'Look after your guest, Jess – never mind the dog!' called Mrs Jameson. 'Poor Lily. You must be frozen!'

But Lily was perfectly happy. Jess was treating her as a member of the family and it felt good. Jess emerged from the kitchen, explaining that fish was Molly's favourite thing. There was a cat in the house that was very fond of it too but, Jess explained, she was hiding.

The living room of Jess's house was big, warm and welcoming. With its comfortable, saggy armchairs, huge wooden table, heaps of books and games, and dog hairs on the carpet, it instantly made Lily feel at home. The fire in the hearth smouldered gently. A basket on the floor was filled with knitting wool and needles, and another overflowed with the parts of a wooden railway set. There was a kitchen on the left and a staircase leading from the middle of the room, and from an open door on the right came a rasping noise that was sometimes musical.

'That's my wee brother Tam learning the violin,' said Jess. 'If you think that's bad, you should have heard him when he started. That's the room where Mum takes her music students. Tam's eight and Lewis is five.'

As she spoke, a small curly-haired boy slid down the banister, jumped off and ran to the basket of wooden railway. ('Hi, Lewis!' called Jess.) Presently the violin stopped groaning and another, slightly bigger boy emerged from the music room and vanished up the stairs. A tortoiseshell cat trotted past him and rubbed against Jess's legs.

'Hello, Pebbles!' said Jess, kneeling to scratch under the cat's uplifted chin. 'She's been hiding. She doesn't like Tam's playing – do you, sweetie? Usually she goes outside when Tam plays, but not when it's like this. You don't like this weather – do you, Pebbles?'

She sat down at the table, pulled a sheet of paper towards her and began drawing a cartoony sort of cat. Pebbles jumped up on to her lap.

'Sometimes the storms go on so long you think you'll never see the sun again,' she said. 'You don't go out unless you have to, so you're cooped up like the hens. We call it cabin fever – you start going round the twist. But you still have to check on the sheep. If it's lambing time you have to get out on the hill to bring the ewes down.'

'Poor sheep!' said Lily.

'They're tough little things,' said Mrs Jameson, who was folding washing. 'They're bred for the hills. We bring them in if we have to.'

'Do the seals get scared when the sea throws them around?' asked Lily.

Jess giggled.

'They're seals!' she said. 'That's how they live! They've got all that roly-poly blubber to keep them warm, so they don't mind what the sea does. That's their life. They just go on with their fishing.'

She finished the cat sketch and began to draw a seal with a happy smile on its face. 'Then again,' she said, 'the seals might be selkie people. The islands are full of stories about the selkies.'

'What's a selkie?' asked Lily.

Jess looked up in surprise. 'Don't they teach you anything in Edinburgh?' she said. 'Selkies are in the old songs and stories. They're seals, but they can be human too. They're human on land and seals in the water. In some of the stories, the selkies have a sealskin that they can take off and put on again. The traditional story goes something like – a man sees a beautiful woman on the beach and falls in love with her, and she tells him she is really a seal and is only human when on land. Anyway, she agrees to marry him, but then she isn't happy because she longs to be in the water again with the other seals. She keeps trying to return. In most of the stories she gets away back to the sea, even if her husband tries to stop her. Sometimes the seal woman brings her sealskin with her and her husband knows that she can't go back to the sea without it, so he hides it, but she always finds it and gets away.'

She finished the picture, added the name 'Shona' underneath, and pushed it across the table to Lily. 'There. Shona the Selkie.'

'I don't think Shona the Selkie wants anyone to fall in love with her,' said Lily. 'She just wants to come and play on the beach with her friends all day, then go back into the water. It's not her fault if a man comes along.'

She took a pencil and drew a rock with seashells round it. 'That's where she's hiding her sealskin,' she said as she sketched. 'The other seals guard it so nobody can take it away.'

They moved upstairs to Jess's room where, for the rest of the morning, they wrote and illustrated stories about Shona the Selkie. Jess said that Molly looked a bit like a selkie when she was swimming so she came into the stories too, playing with the selkie on the shore or, more often, splashing about with her. Jess's windowsill was scattered with shells brought home from walks along the beach, and Lily drew those in the corners of the pages, paying careful attention to the delicate swirls and colours. From Jess's bedroom they could look out over the sea and Lily soon learned that something that looked like a wave or a shadow might be the head of a seal.

'I really want to get out again,' she said, and a thought struck her. 'When you go to school, if it's stormy like this and the boats can't go out, do you get a day off?'

'Depends on the day,' said Jess, and there was something different about her voice. She spoke just a little more quickly than usual, almost as if she wanted to get it out of the way. 'If it happens on a Monday you can't go to school, but if it's a Friday, you can't get home.'

'Can't get home?' repeated Lily, working out what this meant. 'You mean, you stay there for a week at a time?'

'Yes. It's too much travelling to do every day,' said Jess, looking out of the window and not at Lily. 'All the high school students go on the Monday morning boat and come back for the weekend on Friday, so long as we can get through. There's a boarding house to stay in.'

'Like – ' began Lily, then stopped. She had been about to say, 'Like in books?' but stopped herself because she had a feeling that it was the wrong thing to say.

'It's not Hogwarts, if that's what you mean,' said Jess. She gave a tight little laugh without a smile, then changed the subject. 'Do you sometimes go up to the dig with your parents?'

'Oh yes,' said Lily. 'I've been doing that since I was a wee girl. We haven't found anything much at this one, though. Well, not yet.'

'Everybody wash for lunch!' called Jess's mum from downstairs, and they ran down to a meal of bread, oatcakes, salad and cheese at the big wooden table. There were strawberries too, sweet and bright with flavour, just picked from the sheltered garden.

Jess wanted to know about the excavation. So did her brothers, who wanted to know if they'd found any swords, skeletons, pirate treasure or secret tunnels, and whether they were digging up the whole hillside. When Lily – who didn't like disappointing them – admitted that there were only two main trenches and they hadn't found bones in either of them, they lost interest. Jess didn't.

'Are they looking for the Viking princess?' she asked.

Her mother smiled. 'That's just one of those stories,' she said.

'But it might be true,' said Jess. 'Everyone says there were Vikings here once.'

'Dad says they don't know for sure what they'll find,' said Lily. 'There could be anything up there, from any age. Who was this princess?'

'I don't know,' admitted Jess. 'It's just a story, but people say there was a Viking princess who died on the island and was buried here.'

'Yes, but some people say it's a selkie's grave or even a mermaid's,' Mrs Jameson pointed out. 'It's just something they say. When my mum was a little girl they used to say there was a selkie princess buried somewhere near Unfell. Goodness only knows what the truth is.'

Jess looked down at her plate and fidgeted with the strawberry hulls. 'Do you think I might be able to come and have a look at the dig one day?'

'Oh yes!' said Lily, nearly bouncing on her seat. She had been meaning to suggest it – the dig would be a lot more fun with Jess around. 'As soon as the weather gets better, we can go up there. You can help if you like. Every bit of soil has to be checked in case there's anything in it.'

Jess's face brightened with joy. It was funny, thought Lily, that they enjoyed each other's lifestyles so much.

Jess had shown her the lovely beaches and the seals. She could show Jess the dig. And Mum and Dad should know about this Viking princess, even if she never existed.

Unna's story

I heard them talking in low voices when they thought I was asleep. The man who brings the firewood came in and I heard him and Siv whispering. I didn't get it all, but I caught the sound of my own name and listened as hard as I could.

'It's a shame,' said Siv. I felt her hand stroke the top of my head. 'She won't make old bones.'

What did that mean? How can somebody make bones? And if you made them they'd be new bones, wouldn't they? How can you make old bones, and why would you want to? I puzzled about it for a while, but then I fell asleep. This morning had been so exhausting that Magnus had to carry me home from the beach …

It was fine and warm and I begged Siv to let me go out. She had to ask my parents, and they said that I could go, but she must bring me back at once if the wind changed, or if the hard tight breath came upon me, or if I had a pain. She made me wear my woollen cloak, though I didn't want to. It's too hot and it prickles and by the time we got down to the harbour it was making me damp and sweaty, and I hoped, hoped, HOPED that Siv wouldn't notice. If she'd thought I was ill she would have taken me home and made me lie down. But I got away with it, and the morning was so exciting! There were boats in the harbour!

They were trading boats, so my father was sent for. He knew these traders – they've been here before – and he was happy to let them trade here. They had furs and woollen cloth, and some amber jewellery, and soon everyone was crowding around them, including Siv. I took off my cloak and sat on a rock, watching the seals in the bay. They didn't come close while the boats were in, and that's safest for them. The men on the boat would kill them for sealskins and meat.

Siv and my mother glanced at me now and again but they didn't say anything, so I must have looked well. I knew I was well, sitting on a warm rock with the breeze in my face and my feet in a rock pool. The water below my feet was as still and clear as it could be. Looking down into it I could see seaweed forests where the hermit crabs scuttled about, and sea anemones waving their delicate arms.

I heard one of the traders say, 'And what about the little maid there?'

'If you mean the child by the pool, she's Lord Olaf's daughter,' said Siv. 'You'd best be polite about her.'

'Ah, in that case, she should have the best,' he said. 'We have cloth as yellow as her hair and jewellery fit for Olaf's daughter.'

I pretended not to listen, but I did. Siv went to find my father and soon they were bartering. They were talking about the yellow cloth, and I heard my father say the word 'amber'.

Amber is the most beautiful thing! It looks like the clearest honey, but it's as hard as stone. When you look into it, you might see little bits of leaf, or a bubble, or even a tiny insect. It's just like looking into a rock pool and seeing a different world in there. And now I have a piece of amber, all of my own! My father bought it for me! He gave it to me when we got home, and I held it and gazed into it. In the amber I can see a fern like a tiny forest in a drop of gold. There's even silver all round it and a loop so I can wear it. Father gave me a leather band too, to wear it on, but my amber is so new and beautiful that I don't want to wear it yet, only look at it. I held it up to the light to see the sun shine through it.

I wanted to show it to Siv, but she'd gone. I looked in all the huts and couldn't find her so I climbed a hill to get a good view. From there I could see her with other women fetching water, so I ran down to tell her, but I had to stop and get my breath back before I got there.

Siv saw me. She put down her leather bucket and ran to me, calling my name. I tried to tell her I was all right, but I couldn't get the words out and then my legs wouldn't stay up. Siv grabbed me. Somebody said I was turning blue.

They always say that. People aren't blue! I've seen my reflection in rock pools and in the polished bronze mirrors, and I am not blue! But when I get the tight breath, they say I'm blue. Magnus carried me home.

I lay on my bed with my eyes closed and my amber in my hand. I imagined secret worlds in the drop of amber – the secret world of the rock pool and the secret world of the seals under the waves. I imagined being a selkie – a seal princess, swimming with them through underwater forests.

Chapter 4
Storm and Rainbow

For the rest of that day, the wind bent the few trees on the island. It kept the boat away and the chickens sulking in their shed. The next morning Jess's mum collected Lily to spend the day with them, then phoned elderly neighbours to make sure that they had everything they needed. Molly quietly helped herself to socks from the washing basket.

'The very old and very young can't stay on their feet in this weather,' said Mrs Jameson. 'Jess, Lily, will you come with me to do some messages? Edie's ordered her groceries from the shop but she can't get out to collect them. Sheila Lammie can't get out to walk her wee dog, so you might just take him for a quick run up the lane. Then, on the way back, we can pick up Malcolm for his violin lesson.'

'Mrs Lammie's dog is Sammy Lammie,' said Jess as they dashed through the rain to the car. 'He can't run – he can't even walk. He waddles.'

The journey took them rattling along the main road to Ollerswick, the town Lily had seen from the hill. As they drew nearer she saw that it was bigger than she'd thought.

'There's a pedestrian crossing!' she said, and Jess and her mum laughed. 'I didn't know there were any of those on the island!'

'We're quite civilized!' said Jess. 'We've even got shops and a post office!'

'Remember, Jess, Lily arrived by air,' said her mum. 'She hasn't seen this end of the island. If you'd come by boat, Lily, this is where you would have arrived.'

Mrs Jameson parked the car near a small harbour where fishing boats sheltered from the storm. Lily and Jess pulled their hoods forward over their heads and were blown like leaves into the little town. There was a cluster of small streets and a few shops – a paper shop, a chemist, and 'Shepherdson – General Dealer' which, Jess said, sold everything from paints to pants. A brightly painted cafe had the sign 'Coffee and Craft' outside the door and displayed intricately knitted sweaters in the window.

'Mum knits for them,' said Jess. 'Lots of people on the island make things to sell in there. Jewellery and cards and things. And paintings.'

They hurried past a garage, which also sold everything that farmers were likely to need, an inn and a squat little church built of weathered red stone. Its gravestones stood to attention around it, though some of them had fallen over. Opposite was a simple, modern building.

'That's the community hall,' said Jess. 'It's got everything. It opened the year I started school and they had a big opening ceremony with the newspapers and the council, and even our Member of the Scottish Parliament came over for it, and there was a ribbon cutting ceremony. They wanted the youngest child in the school to cut the ribbon, and that was me. I saw my picture in the paper and thought I was famous!'

'You were!' said her mother. 'You were island-famous. In a place this small, everyone gets the chance to be famous.'

'I never knew any of this was here!' said Lily. 'The lady who owns the cottage filled up the cupboards and the fridge for us before we got here. And Mum and Dad wouldn't come if they didn't have to. I mean, they wouldn't come here just to look round – they want to get on with the dig.' Not for the first time, she thought that her parents were more interested in dead towns than living ones, but she didn't like to say so.

They hurried into a shop where Mrs Jameson delivered eggs and collected the groceries. She chatted for a while with the man at the counter, then thought of something.

'I'd best buy some batteries while we're here,' she said.

'Mum, we've got a box full of them!' exclaimed Jess.

'Even so,' said her mum. 'It's no good waiting until we need them. You'll want some for your torch when you go off to school, Jess.'

Jess made a bit of a face at that, and didn't speak as they battled against the wind back to the car. When Mrs

Jameson stopped at a cottage on the edge of the village, Jess ran out to deliver the box of groceries to a stooped old lady who came to the door in a flowery crossover apron and fluffy slippers. Then there was the stout little dog, 'Sheila Lammie's Sammy', to be taken for a waddle up the lane and back.

'Is it always like this?' Lily asked as Jess clambered into the car again. 'Running errands for people?'

'Doesn't everyone do that?' replied Jess, and twisted round in her seat. 'If you look down from here, you see that white building behind the church? That's my school – I mean, my old school.'

Jess went on gazing at the school until it was out of sight. *Almost as if she were hungry for it,* thought Lily, and felt sad for Jess.

'It'll be strange, won't it, going to school on the mainland?' she said, but Jess was still looking out of the window and didn't seem to hear. Lily nearly asked again, but decided not to.

There was one more stop on the way home.

'This is where we pick Malcolm up,' explained Jess. 'He's got a violin lesson with Mum today. Mum says he's so good there's not much she can teach him, but he still has lessons with her in the holidays.'

Malcolm turned out to be about fourteen, tall, with black hair and a kind, squarish face. Clambering into the car, he asked Jess if she was looking forward to high school. Jess shrugged.

I really need to talk to Jess about school, thought Lily. *Even if she doesn't want to.*

* * *

After yet another day of wind and rain, Lily understood what Jess meant about 'cabin fever'. The only milk left in the cottage was the long-life kind which she didn't like, so she ate dry cereal for breakfast. Damp socks steamed gently in front of the fire. Again, Jess's parents invited Lily's family for a meal and this time they accepted. They set out wearing waterproofs, but as they walked the rain stopped, the sky cleared and, to everyone's surprise, the sun began to break through.

'Oh wow, oh look, *look!*' Lily cried, and stood still.

A rainbow, the biggest and clearest she had ever seen in her life, arched high above the sea. Another, paler one appeared under it. For a while, all three of them stood gazing up into the sky – then a hare bolted out from a gorse bush with its long legs kicking up behind it and took off across the moors and Lily jumped, and they all laughed.

'We can finally get back to the dig tomorrow,' said Dad as they walked on. 'It's been frustrating, not being able to work. We'd just started finding interesting stuff when we had to stop.'

'Really?' said Lily. 'Viking stuff?'

'Nothing so far back,' said Dad. 'Medieval.'

'But were there Vikings here?' persisted Lily.

'We can't say for definite,' said Dad. 'Tradition says that there were, but it's strange – there are no documents to prove it, and no evidence of Viking occupation.'

'No evidence *yet*,' said Mum.

'Maybe they weren't here for long, and didn't leave any evidence,' said Lily. Her parents seemed to find this very funny, but it made perfect sense to her.

She was here, thought Lily. Looking up at the rainbow, she felt absolutely sure of it. *Jess's Viking princess, or whoever she was – she did exist. She stood here, just where I'm standing, and saw rainbows.*

* * *

At Jess's house, Molly bounded to the door to meet them. The room smelt deliciously of casserole and wood smoke. The boys, who had been making a den under the table, looked out, said hello and disappeared again until they were ordered to go and wash.

Over the meal – which tasted wonderful even though Lily knew they were eating one of the lambs reared on the island – the adults talked about the dig at Unfell, Jess and Lily made plans for the next few days, and Jess was just saying, 'Dad, tell them about – ' when the lights went out.

'That's a surprise!' said her mum. 'That usually happens during the storm, not after it! Never mind – everything's cooked that needs to be cooked and we're used to power cuts here. There you are, Jess, I told you we'd need batteries. We'll get the generator going if we have to.'

'It won't get dark for hours,' said Jess. 'Not at this time of year.'

When they had finished eating, Jess's mum lit candles and everybody sat around the fire with warm drinks. The two boys took a torch and disappeared under the table again, and Jess and Lily curled up together in an armchair to read a book called *Warrior Scarlet*. They'd both read it before, but they knew they'd enjoy it even more the second time round. The conversation drifted past them, but presently Lily found she was listening.

'There's never been reliable evidence of Viking life on the island,' her father was saying. 'Small artefacts have been found, things like jewellery and pottery, but they might have been left behind by northern trading ships selling to whoever lived here. Viking traders went everywhere. However, there's a strong local tradition that there were Viking settlements here, so there might be some truth in it. The name of the little town at the harbour – Ollerswick – that sounds Scandinavian to me, and there's a legend that a famous Viking leader lived here. Olaf Harraldson, or Elkskull, as he was called.'

'Elk Skull!' repeated Jess.

'I think I've heard of him,' said Mrs Jameson.

'Oh yes,' said Lily's dad. 'There are lots of tales about Olaf Elkskull, but there are gaps in his life story. He was known as Elkskull because he killed a gigantic elk and made a trophy from its skull. It must have scared the daylights out of his enemies. There are sagas and poems about him –

Olaf brought the beast down and bore it homeward
Skilled smiths took the skull, set it in silver
He hoisted it in battle, high over helmets.'

'Cool!' said two voices from under the table.

'Why did he kill it?' asked Jess.

'Good question,' said Lily's dad. 'In those days there was a lot more hunting for food, but maybe it was a rogue elk and it had harmed somebody. Olaf was very famous – he left Norway because he was driven out by his brother, and went into exile for years. He could have been here, but there's no evidence.'

'But there *might* have been a princess!' insisted Jess.

'Jess, are you sure you want the princess's grave to be found?' asked her mum. 'I've always liked the uncertainty. As long as we don't know what really happened, we can make up stories about her. She might never have existed. She might just be a story, like the selkies.'

'Yes, but selkies aren't real and Vikings are – I mean, were!' said Jess, and suddenly they were all laughing, and the lights came on, and Molly looked up and beat her tail on the hearthrug. Lewis complained that it was more exciting with the lights off and he'd wanted to go to bed in the dark. Then Lily's mum looked at her watch and said how late it was, and that it was time to go back to the cottage.

'And if anyone wants to see the dig,' she added, 'just turn up at the site in the morning.'

'Yes, please!' said Jess. 'See you in the morning, Lily! It's always fun the morning after a storm. There's all kinds of driftwood and washed glass pebbles lying around on the shore. And sometimes a few boulders if the cliffs crumble a bit.'

'The cliffs crumble?' repeated Lily.

'Oh, just a wee bit,' shrugged Jess. 'Don't worry. Your house won't fall in.'

* * *

Lily's Diary

I can't sleep. There's too much in my head and it's not just about selkies and princesses. The Viking princess is in the past, if she ever existed. It's Jess that I have to think about. She's unhappy about school and doesn't want to talk about it.

Talking would help, but I don't know how to get her to do that if she doesn't want to. I don't want to do anything that would make her unhappy or push her away. We're friends, and I don't want to spoil that.

Lily fell asleep that night thinking about Jess and high school. When she woke up she was still thinking about it, but now she knew what to do, as if her brain had sorted it out for her while she slept. *Jess is worried about high school. So am I, but in a different way. So that's the way in. Don't ask her if she's worried about school. Tell her that* I *am. Now I have to choose the right moment.*

She got up and dressed quickly, ready to go to the dig.

Chapter 5
Unna of the Seals

Unna's story

When I was little, some of my father's men went down to the shore to kill seals for meat and fur, and when I found out about that I couldn't stop crying. It was like slaughtering my friends! What if they were selkie people? The thought of it made me vomit, and the pain and tight breath came upon me so hard that I couldn't breathe at all. I remember my mother bending to listen to my heart before I passed out, and I came round again to see her gazing down at me with fear in her face. The bitter smell of Siv's medicines was all around me.

After that, my father ordered that the seals must not be killed. He said that we have sheep and goats enough, and deer and hares can be killed, but not seals. The killing of the seals had made his child gravely ill, and Unna Olafsdatter must not be ill!

A ship came in this morning. It was a longship this time, not a trader. Father and his men were ready with weapons and armour, but there was no need to fight. The ship brought some of his friends from the north lands, and they had news for us.

I already knew that my parents used to live far away in the north lands, before they came here. Today I found out why they went away.

My father had an older brother, Lars, who hated and feared him. More than once he tried to kill Father, Mother and me and all the household too. The last time, he sent men to burn down Father's hall with everyone in it! It was too dangerous to stay any longer, so we all sailed here.

The news now is that my Uncle Lars is dead and he had no children to inherit his lands, so it all goes to Father. My parents can go home and claim what is theirs – but why would they want to? We have our island, like a bright green jewel in a silver sea. On clear days the sea sparkles as if the stars had come to play in it.

After the rain today I walked uphill, with Siv heaving along behind me, grumbling at me to slow down, ready to grab me and carry me if she thought I might be ill. When I could climb no further I turned to look down at the cluster of huts and my father's hall. Smoke was drifting up from cooking fires and the rainbow bridge shone in the sky. The seals bobbed about in the water or sprawled on the rocks, as if they knew they were safe.

I hope they do. I watched them, and thought – do you know you are safe? Do you know that I saved you? I am Unna Olafsdatter and I have made this island a place of peace for you. If I ever become famous and the bards sing songs about me, I will be Unna of the Seals. Even if we go to my father's lands over the sea, my heart will be here, with the seals.

Lily, who had been sick to death of the dig before, didn't mind going back now that Jess was there too. Besides, just before the storms began the team had started to find interesting things instead of bits of old teapot. (At least, they'd found interesting things in Trench One. Nothing much had turned up in Trench Two.) Jess had arrived and was keen to help, so Lily explained to her about sifting soil and using a trowel, and what to do with pottery, bones, glass and any other signs of human life. They were dusting off bits of animal bone with toothbrushes when Jess looked up and said, 'There's Malcolm!'

Lily turned to see Malcolm, the violin student, sitting on the edge of a trench and talking to some of the team. He heard his name and waved.

'Hi Jess!' he called. 'Isn't this good?'

Lily soon found out that some of the archaeology team were staying with Malcolm's family – like everybody else on the island they did several jobs, one of which was running a guest house. The team had invited Malcolm to the dig and his broad smile showed how much he was enjoying it. In his hands was something that looked like a big and very rusty nail, and he held it out to Lily's mum.

'Dr Walker, is this anything important?' he asked.

Lily's mum pushed dusty hands through her hair,

peered at the object, held it up to the light, brushed it and examined it under a lens. Everyone waited.

'It's a nail,' she said firmly, and Malcolm looked a bit disappointed until she added, 'twelfth century, maybe a bit earlier,' and he cheered up at once.

'That's ancient!' he said, gazing at the nail as she handed it back to him. 'I'm holding something which is nearly a thousand years old!'

'But it isn't old enough!' said Jess. 'It isn't from the Vikings!'

'Archaeology goes in layers,' explained Lily. 'This might be the medieval layer, but there could be a Viking layer underneath. And even if we don't find anything Viking, it doesn't mean that they weren't here, because we're only exploring this little bit – we can't dig up the whole island. We might just be looking in the wrong place.'

'We might just be rubbish archaeologists,' said Dad.

'Then we have to find the right place!' said Jess and giggled. 'It could be under your cottage!'

'It could be under your henhouse!' said Lily, and they laughed a lot about digging up the school, the church, the hall and 'Shepherdson – General Dealer' in the search for Vikings.

* * *

Later that morning the next boat came in, so not much work was done in the afternoon. Jess, Lily and at least half the team went into the little town on the harbour to stock up with milk, bread, beans, fruit, sweets, torch batteries and toilet rolls.

Jess and Lily bought notebooks to write stories in, then sat in the cafe drinking milkshakes while Molly lay under the table.

'You know ... ' said Lily, then stopped, thought, and started again, 'you know about ... about high school?'

Jess made a face and said nothing.

Lily tried to think of something clever to say, failed, and blurted out, 'I don't want to go there. I mean ... I mean ... they make you play rugby!'

A splutter of giggles ran down Jess's straw and bubbles jumped in her milkshake.

'And the uniform's green,' went on Lily. 'I'll look like a cabbage!'

Jess let go of the straw and sat back in her chair, still laughing.

'Is that all?' she said. 'Rugby and a green sweater?'

'Oh, and, you know,' said Lily vaguely, 'new lessons, new teachers, getting lost, all of that.' Then she added, 'What about you?'

Jess stopped laughing and picked up her glass again. The milkshake sank further down in the glass.

'It's all right, I suppose,' she said, and shrugged.

'No, it isn't,' said Lily, and leaned across the table towards her. 'You don't want to go, do you?'

Jess looked into her glass.

'I don't like to think about it,' she said. There was a pause, then in a lower voice she added, 'I get upset if I think about it.'

They finished their drinks without saying much, then walked down to the harbour.

After some silent seal watching, Jess said, 'I've lived all my life on this island. I mean, of course I've been to the mainland for shopping and holidays and things and it's OK. I just don't want to have to live away from home.'

She pulled up a few tufts of weeds and flicked them towards the sea. A hard edge came into her voice.

'I don't want to go – I don't want to leave my family and I don't see why anyone should force me to! It's not right! I don't want to go into a boarding house and share a room with somebody I don't know! You know what it's like in a new school! You're worrying about rugby and uniform, but at the end of the school day you can go home and get away from it! You can sit down with your mum and dad and tell them if anything's bothering you, and sleep in your own bed with all your own things around you!'

Lily felt she ought to say something, but didn't know what. Jess went on in a tight, strained voice that sounded like she was near to tears.

'My brothers drive me round the bend but they're still my brothers and they're funny. And I'll miss Molly and Pebbles and the hens, and – ' Jess didn't say 'Mum and Dad'. She just folded her lips tightly and went on flicking bits of grass at the water.

Lily gave her some time, then said, 'Have you talked to your mum and dad about it?'

Jess nodded. 'They just say that everyone feels like that when they start high school, but it's all right when you get there,' she said quickly, as if she wanted to get the words out before she cried. 'Mum grew up on the island, and she had to go to school on the mainland. But there were more kids on the island then. This year, I'm the only one going up.'

Viciously she wrenched up a fistful of dandelions and flung them at the sea, then turned to walk away with Lily following.

Quite suddenly Jess stopped and turned to her with a smile.

'Who cares?' she said. 'It's the summer holiday and it's sunny and I've got a new friend, so I'm going to make the most of it.'

'Me too,' said Lily firmly, as Jess clearly wanted to change the subject. 'What shall we do? Go down to the beach, or write stories?'

'Write stories on the beach,' said Jess, so they did.

Chapter 6
Dancing the Reels

There were many more sunny days after that. Jess and Lily spent hours together, writing and illustrating their books of stories, helping at the dig, watching seals, splashing about on the shore with Molly and walking for what must have been miles around the island. Lily became familiar with the sandy bays, the soft, springy turf and the rough, rocky uphill climbs. There were more deer to be seen, and hares, and nimble little red squirrels. The girls stayed well away from the cliff edges. On some of the beaches there were sandstone boulders where parts of the cliff had fallen away.

'There are rabbit warrens in the cliff faces,' said Jess. 'And that weakens them, so when there's a real storm – not like the one we had the other night, I mean a *real* storm – the waves can make the cliffs crumble, and when the underneath starts to give way, so does the top.'

'How bad can a storm be?' asked Lily.

'Stay here long enough and you'll find out,' said Jess.

* * *

On wet days they would sometimes put on waterproofs, go to the dig, and crouch under the makeshift shelters which covered the trenches. The dig was getting interesting. Everybody became very excited about half a sandal and some bits of decorated silver that might have been part of a plate.

'We're looking at a monastery here,' said Dad as the team crowded round to see.

'Or a nunnery,' said Mum.

'How old?' asked Lily.

Dad frowned down at the sandal as if he wanted it to talk to him.

'At a guess, anything between the twelfth and fourteenth centuries,' he said. 'We'll know more when we've got further and found more.'

'Still no Vikings?' said Lily.

'Sorry to disappoint you!' said Dad. 'But we have to find out what's here, not what we *want* to be here.'

Lily thought this sounded very wise. All the same, she still wanted Vikings, if only for Jess's sake. She nearly asked, 'Are you *sure* you're looking in the right place?' but then remembered that her parents had been digging things up since long before she was born, and didn't say anything at all. Jess came to see what they were looking at.

'Only one sandal?' she said. 'Maybe he was a one-legged monk. Mum said to ask you, do you want to come to the ceilidh[1] on Friday?'

---

[1] Ceilidh is pronounced 'kayly'. It's a Scottish word for a party, usually with traditional music and dancing.

'I didn't know there was a ceilidh,' said Dad.

'I did,' said Lily. 'There are posters in the shop windows in town.'

'We have a ceilidh on one Friday every month in the hall,' Jess told them. 'It's great – everybody goes. There's dancing and music, and it's an open mic – anyone can sing or play if they want to. Bring your flute, Lily. Mum and Dad always do some music, and Malcolm plays, and there's supper, so don't have anything to eat before you come. You should all come. It starts at eight and goes on until everyone's gone home. Oh, and Mum says, can we take Molly out this afternoon?'

* * *

'Do you suppose he wore that elk skull on his head?' asked Jess as they walked Molly across the broad meadow above Jess's house. 'He could have kept it as a spare helmet.'

They had been discussing what Dad had said about the Viking leader, Olaf Elkskull, and his killing of a giant elk. The sun was bright, but the breeze was so fierce on their faces that they tried walking backwards. Their hair blew into their eyes so they couldn't see.

'Elks are massive,' said Lily. 'I went with Mum and Dad to a dig in Sweden and we saw an elk in the wild. They had skulls in the museum too. They're much too big for helmets. It would be like putting a grown-up hat on your wee Lewis – he wouldn't be able to see.'

Jess shaded her eyes as she looked out to sea. 'Pity,' she said. 'I love the idea of an elk-skull helmet. Lily, look! There are seals in the bay. Shall we go and see them, when Molly's run her energy off?'

They turned downhill, weaving their way between gorse and heather. Below them, the sea glittered. Lily imagined longships carving the water in two as they headed relentlessly to the beach.

'People draw pictures of Vikings with horns on their helmets, but that isn't real,' she said. 'They had plain helmets. Horns would be a nuisance. If Olaf went into battle with an elk skull on his head he'd get his antlers caught on the trees.'

After that, there was a lot of giggling about Olaf Elkskull getting his antlers stuck, or sliced off with a battleaxe, and what on earth was an elk skull useful for, even if you did cover it with gold and silver? Lily thought he might have used it as a coat rack, Jess said he could have hung his washing on it, and Molly lolloped around them until they were near the beach and she found a rabbit to chase.

'She never catches them,' said Jess. 'There are rabbit warrens all over the island, even in the cliffs, so the place is teeming with them, but Molly has never caught one yet.

She ran headlong into one and it still got away. And if she did catch one, she wouldn't know what to do with it. Molly, here! Sit still while we get your lead on. Good girl. Where were we up to?'

'The great Olaf using his elk skull as a washing line,' said Lily. 'He walked about with his favourite Viking socks blowing from the antlers. Ones with frilly tops.'

'Frilly!' exclaimed Jess.

'All right then, hairy, tickly ones,' conceded Lily. 'Come to think of it, he might have used it as something to frighten his enemies, so he could have carried it into battle.'

'Did he take the washing off it first?' asked Jess, and they rolled laughing on the grass and heather while Molly thought this was a new game and tried to join in. They picked themselves up and ran the rest of the way down to the sandy little bay.

The sun warmed the bay and the cliff shielded it from the wind. A seal basking on the rocks raised its head to look at them, then lost interest and settled down. Lily walked along the sand, picking up pebbles. She liked the pale oval ones with flecks of colour and the smooth washed glass like transparent green beads. When she had enough, she sat down and made patterns with them on the sand, and presently Jess came to join her.

'Do you remember, yesterday,' said Lily, looking at the pebbles and not at Jess, 'when we were talking about high school? Have you seen where you're going to be staying yet?'

'Ach yes, I went on a visit,' said Jess. 'There are two or three beds to a room, and they're big rooms. You can put your own pictures on the walls and everything.' She fidgeted with the pebbles. 'Please don't say, "That'll be nice" or anything like that. It wouldn't matter if they moved me to Buckingham Palace. It's not on the island, and that's what matters. Molly and Pebbles won't understand. They'll think I've walked out on them.'

'Then they'll soon work out that you'll walk in again every Friday night,' said Lily.

'Yes, but what about the Fridays when I don't?' said Jess. 'When the weather's really bad, everyone has to stay on the mainland. I don't want that!' She folded her lips tightly and concentrated on the pebbles.

'You must know some of the people who are there already,' suggested Lily.

'This year it's just me going up and last year, there was nobody,' said Jess. 'The year before that there were the three lads, Ben, Patrick and Malcolm– that's Malcolm who plays the violin. They're all two years older than me, and all boys – they stick together. I can't hang around with them. Then there are four girls in the sixth form.'

Lily wanted to tell her that it would be all right, but she didn't. *How do I know if it'll be all right or not?*

On the damp sand the turning tide had left a stem of seaweed, long and thick like a snake and gleaming wet. Its leafy fronds trailed around it. Lily ran to it, heaved it up with both hands and held it dripping over her head.

'Look at me!' she called. 'I'm Olaf Elfskull!'

Jess laughed. 'You're getting wet! You're Silly Lily Seaweedskull!'

'That's Princess Silly Lily Seaweedskull!' proclaimed Lily and they went home laughing and starting a new story about the adventures of Reginald Rabbitskull the Very Small Viking and Silly Lily Seaweedskull. School was an awkward subject and they had to be careful how they talked about that, but they could say anything about Vikings. At Jess's, they made an elk skull out of cardboard and coathangers and hung washing on it, and Molly stole the socks.

* * *

The dig was now demanding all of Mum and Dad's attention. They only had another two weeks on the island and new finds were emerging every day. More sandals had turned up, as well as pottery and some seeds that Dad found fascinating. He spent a lot of time peering at them under a lens, photographing them and comparing them with pictures of things that had been found on other digs. When they found broken bowls and flasks, he examined them to find out what had been kept in them.

'We'll have to get these analysed,' he said, putting on plastic gloves so that he could push the seeds around and turn them over. 'These must have been medicines. The only valuable things we've found in this trench are those bits of silver. There's no money and no jewellery, just a lot of pottery and these seeds. It could well be a monastery hospital and a graveyard. Didn't I say, Lily, there might be a graveyard? The earth on this island is very peaty, which is good, because peat preserves things.'

'What sort of things?' asked Jess. 'Bodies?'

'All sorts of things,' said Lily quickly, because she was used to seeing skeletons but Jess wasn't.

Mum was sitting on the ground doing a jigsaw with pottery.

'There's the second trench as well,' she said, 'the one up the hill. But we haven't found much there yet so we'll concentrate on this one. Anyway, we should clear up for now. I could do with a soak in the bath before the ceilidh.'

***

If Lily and her family hadn't known where the hall was, they could have just followed the crowd. Groups of people from all over the island drifted towards the hall door. *It's like walking into a funnel,* thought Lily. Whole families arrived together, and all ages, from five-year-old Lewis to ninety-year-old Edie with her walking stick. Some people dressed casually in T-shirts and jeans, some of the women wore summer dresses and a lot of the men, including Jess's dad, were in kilts. The band had begun to play and lilting traditional tunes danced out from the open door.

'It looks amazing!' whispered Mum as they walked into the hall.

Lily found herself in a high-ceilinged hall painted in pale yellow and white with a plain wooden floor. Chairs had been laid out in little clusters, pretty curtains were tied back at the windows and fairy lights hung above the stage.

Jess's little brother Tam saw Lily and rushed into the next room shouting, 'Jess, your friend's here!' and soon Jess was running to meet her.

'Come and see!' said Jess. She grabbed Lily's hand and whisked her off to show her the next room.

'We're setting out the supper in here,' she said, hurrying past trays of crusty bread and salad. She dragged Lily on into the kitchen, which smelled of jacket potatoes, chicken, and apple pie. Busy people in aprons covered dishes with crisply ironed tea towels and fussed around an enormous cooking range. Jess pulled her into yet another room.

'This is the meeting room,' she said, 'and sometimes it's the library.' She went on whisking Lily from one room to the next. 'This is where they store everything, and that's where they keep the playgroup things, and the toilets are here. There's a disabled loo and a proper baby change place – we fundraised for those at school. And look at this – this is new!'

She opened the door to what looked like an office, with desks and computers.

'It's the Island Hub,' she explained. 'Most people on the island have computers now – you need one out here, especially if you do online selling. My mum and her friends sell their hand-knitted sweaters online. But for people who don't have a computer, they can come and use one of these. The post lady teaches IT courses here and she's setting up an island website. The next thing is, we're going to build an extension for a Games Room. Don't you think it's amazing?'

'It is,' agreed Lily, but it wasn't the hall that amazed her. It was Jess. It was funny, in a very nice way, that somebody her own age could be so proud of the local hall. Lily felt like that about her own home, but not about the hall where she went to Guides and dance classes.

'What are you smiling about?' asked Jess.

'You – and this place!' she said, and then someone began playing a tune that made rhythms skip into their feet and they danced into the main hall, linking arms, twirling round each other, turning under, making it up as they went along, and soon everyone was up and dancing with everyone else.

Lily wanted that evening to last for ever. There was music all night – music to make you dance and music to make you stand still and listen. Jess's parents played. Somebody lent Lily's dad a guitar and he sang a song he and some other archaeologists had made up about digging things up in the rain. Jess begged Lily to play her flute, but all the other musicians were so good that she didn't feel confident enough. Malcolm played folk tunes with such joy that everyone was on their feet again, dancing or just clapping or jigging up and down on the spot. There was a raffle of simple prizes that people had given – a fruit hamper, chocolates, a home-made cake – and when it was time for supper, Lily fully understood why Jess had told them not to eat beforehand. Mounds of jacket potatoes, plates full of chicken and bowls piled high with cheese and oatcakes appeared as if by magic. Tea towels were whisked away to reveal so many cakes, fruit pies, trifles and little chocolatey things that Lily had to try hard not to stare.

'Is it always like this?' asked Lily.

Jess thought for a moment. 'It usually is,' she said, 'except we have all the special things at Hogmanay and

Christmas and neeps and haggis for Burns Night, all that sort of thing. But mostly it's like this.'

Lily wondered what the island was like in winter, especially at Christmas and Hogmanay. When they had eaten they walked out into the calm summer evening and the sea-scented air. Jess's little brothers came running from the hall with aeroplanes they had made out of paper plates. Malcolm, with a glass of lemonade in his hand, was chatting to some of his friends.

'I love this island!' said Lily.

'Best place in the world,' agreed Jess. 'I was wanting to ask you – what's Edinburgh like at Hogmanay?'

'I was wondering what it's like here!' said Lily. 'It depends whereabouts in Edinburgh. Hogmanay in the city centre is very busy, so we never go there. There are thousands of people in the streets – sometimes about eighty thousand – with processions and fireworks and dancers, and there are stages set up with bands playing. At home we just visit friends, like everyone else.'

'We mostly come here,' said Jess. 'Everybody does. We have a big party.'

'It's not just Hogmanay in Edinburgh, it's the whole of December,' said Lily. 'We sometimes go into the city after school, when it's getting dark, and it's just – like something from a story. Everything's bright and sparkly!

There are lights all the way down the Royal Mile, and fairgrounds with galloping horses and a big wheel and all that, and an ice rink, and market stalls, just like the ones you see on television, selling sweets and decorations and ... I can't describe it – you have to see it!'

'I'd love that!' said Jess.

'You have to come!' insisted Lily. 'Come and stay with us! Ask your mum and dad, or I'll get my mum and dad to ask them!'

'Do you really think – ' began Jess, then called, 'Tam! Pick that up!'

'I was just going to!' shouted Tam, chasing after a paper plate that had escaped from him and was blowing across the ground. It occurred to Lily that she'd never seen litter on the island.

Then Jess's mum came out and called, 'Jess, Ben, Patrick, you're playing next! Come and get tuned up!'

'See you,' said Jess, and went back into the hall with Malcolm's two friends.

Malcolm stood alone, leaning against the wall with his glass in his hand. Lily walked over to him, feeling a bit shy and hoping he wouldn't think she was silly.

'Malcolm, can I ask you about something?' she asked.

'Ask away,' said Malcolm.

'You know,' she said, feeling a bit awkward, 'well, you know Jess is starting high school in August?'

'Yes, I know,' he said.

Lily crossed her fingers and hoped that Malcolm was as nice as she thought he was.

'The thing is, Jess is ... um ... she sort of—'

'Is she in a stooshie about starting school?' asked Malcolm.

Thank goodness for that, thought Lily. 'Yes, that's what I wanted to tell you,' she said. 'She's worried.'

'Aye, everyone feels like that,' he said. 'She'll be fine.'

'People keep telling her that, but she's still in a stooshie,' said Lily.

Malcolm laughed. 'It's true,' he said. 'She really will be fine! Maybe not straight away, but it soon comes right. When I first went I lay awake the night before, and there were three of us going, not just one like Jess. The only reason I didn't cry the first night at school was that my mates were there. Tell Jess not to fash herself. She might be a wee bit homesick at first. She'll be homesick when she goes back after the first holiday. Everybody is. But it gets better, and we're all there for each other. We'll all be there for Jess. You tell her that the island kids are like family – and she'll make her own friends too. You tell her that.'

'Thanks,' she said, and added, 'it's better if she doesn't know I've talked to you.'

'If you like,' he said, and shrugged. 'But we'll all be her big brothers, Ben and Patrick and me.'

Jess appeared at the door. 'You coming?' she called.

'Sure!' said Malcolm.

'In a second!' called Lily. There was still something she wanted to know.

'What about weekends when you can't get home?' she asked. 'Isn't that really hard?'

'Maybe just at first,' admitted Malcolm. 'But we make the most of it. In winter we all go to a wee cafe at the harbour for hot chocolate, and go bowling, or watch a film or something. It's fine. Here, we should go in or we'll be in trouble with Jess. Have you found anything at the dig?'

* * *

The music went on. Jess and her friends played, Malcolm played again, the band played and there was more dancing. There were fast, breathless reels where Lily lost her place time and again, but the more she got lost the funnier it was, and Jess pushed and pulled her into place. Mum won chocolates in the raffle and Jess's little brothers took a supply of snacks and disappeared under the table. The ceilidh was still going on when Lily and her family went home.

'You'll sleep well tonight,' said Mum.

'I won't,' said Lily. 'I'll think about it all night.'

And that's what she did. She lay awake, reliving the dancing, the music, the friendship and the hope – *oh please, please may it work* – that she had done something to help Jess.

In the morning a gale was whipping its way across the island, so she and Jess spent the day indoors writing a story which now included a selkie ceilidh where seals danced, played the fiddle and ate fish by the bucketful. It was in the evening when Lily's parents dropped their bombshell.

Chapter 7
Run

They ate dinner late that evening, then lit the log fire and Mum passed the chocolates round. Lily had the feeling that her parents were working their way up to something because they were trying too hard to behave normally.

Then Mum took a sip of her coffee and said, 'We've got less than two weeks left on the island now. You've loved it, haven't you, Lily?'

Lily had been trying not to think about that. She was having too much fun to think of leaving. But it wouldn't be the first time she'd had to leave a dig, or a holiday. This time last year she'd had a great time in Wales with a lot of other archaeologists' families, and the year before that she'd cried when they had to leave Denmark. But, for Lily, home was best. She loved the familiarity of sleeping in her own room, in her own bed, and the excitement of meeting up with her friends again and swapping stories of what they'd been doing. She loved her home.

'I didn't think I'd like it here until I met Jess,' she said. 'We're going to keep in touch. Can she come to stay with us? Maybe at half-term?'

'Mum and I have been talking about things,' said Dad. 'We all like it here. You've got a new friend. We've all made friends and there's still a lot of work to be done on this site. So the thing is, sweetheart, Mum and I are thinking of moving to the island.' He leaned forward, his dark eyes twinkling. 'What do you think? Would you like to live here?'

A cold shiver ran through Lily. Yes, she was happy here and Jess would be a lifelong friend. She felt at home in Jess's house. Yes, the island was beautiful, and the ceilidh had been fun. But to live here, in this quiet corner, a world away from Edinburgh? To be cut off every time there was a storm? Leaving behind almost everyone she knew and her favourite places? She wanted to explain, but it was like the day in the cafe when she'd tried to talk to Jess about high school and couldn't find the right words. This time, the only word she could find was, 'No.'

'No?' said her parents, glancing at each other.

'No!' she repeated. 'I don't want to move here!'

'But you love it here!' said Mum. 'You've been so happy!'

'I am, but it's the summer holidays – it isn't home!' insisted Lily. 'Edinburgh's home! Anyway, what would you do? You've got students to teach – you can't keep going back and forth between here and Edinburgh!'

'We talked about that,' said Dad. 'We can make it work. We're being paid for our work on the dig and we both have books we want to write. We could do less teaching and more writing. And we can teach online.'

'We'd do lots of different jobs, like everybody else on the island,' smiled Mum happily. 'That would be a great way to live. Do you think, Lily, we should just try it? You've been so happy here, and there's Jess ... '

Tears stung in Lily's eyes. She really would miss Jess when she went home, but ...

'But I don't belong here!' she insisted. 'And neither do you! How can you think of it? I've just started to feel all right about going to high school and now you say you want me to stay here!'

'We thought it would make you happy!' said Mum.

'You don't *know*!' snapped Lily, and anger too strong to control poured out of her. 'You're always in a trench! You're always digging things up – you have no idea what I want!' She was on her feet now, brushing angry tears from her face. 'You're only interested in dead people and your disgusting ancient hospital! If I were a grubby old skeleton you'd be interested in me! You haven't a clue!'

She ran to the door, pushed her feet into her shoes and grabbed her coat.

'Where are you going?' called Mum.

'Out!' she shouted back. 'Leave me alone!'

She ran and ran with the wind driving her, over the turf, past the gorse bushes, up hills and down them again until her chest hurt with running and she had to stop and gulp down the air. She'd go down to Jackie's Bay – that was her favourite place on the island. Yes, she'd go there, though the wind was against her.

She pulled her coat tightly round herself, lowered her head, and fought her way down the Slidie to the sand. There she found the shelter of a rock where she could huddle down and cry.

She wasn't just crying for herself. She was crying for Jess too.

If I stayed ... if I stayed here ... if I stayed here, Jess would love that. We'd go on the way we do now. She wouldn't be the only one going to that school – we'd go together and live in the boarding house all week, or two weeks if we couldn't get home.

But I don't think I could stand it. I want to go home. And if I go home, I'm abandoning Jess to get on however she can. The thought of it brought more tears to her eyes.

I should stay for Jess.

I can't stay.

What a rubbish friend I am.

She rubbed her face dry, walked down to the water's edge and picked up a stone to skim, but she was too angry to do it well and it sank. She found another and was about to try again when she stopped to watch a domed shape bobbing in the waves.

She put down the stone. The sleek shape disappeared among the waves and appeared again. Yes, it was a seal, and Lily felt calmer as she watched it. She thought of how pleasant it would be to be a seal, with nothing to do but swim and catch fish.

Now that the seal had calmed her, she realized three things. Firstly, she was shivering with cold. Secondly, she was tired. Thirdly, the weather was worse.

The sky was growing darker and a light rain spat into her face. She didn't know how long she'd been out, but she guessed that it must be at least an hour. The tide was coming in. Lily turned and clambered back up the Slidie, her feet slipping and the sea spray flying against her ankles.

On the Braid the wind blew more fiercely and there was no shelter from the rising storm. The rain grew wilder and heavier until it was hard for her to see far in front of her. She hesitated, turning one way and then the other because she was no longer sure of the way home, and fought to put her feet on ...

... on what? On whatever was under her feet, and she was sure it wasn't the path. It wasn't any sort of path. She turned slowly, holding her hair to stop it blowing in her eyes, but she could see no landmarks at all.

Go forward, she thought. *Keep walking away from the sea. I think I should be going uphill but I'm not, so where am I going?*

The dense grey rain fell relentlessly, soaking steadily through her jeans. Was somebody calling her name?

'Lily! Lil-lee!'

Whose voice was that and where did it come from? How near, how far? A figure stood in the mists.

It must be the princess, thought Lily hazily. *The selkie, or the Viking, or whatever she was. She's out there – she's running – is she trying to run back to the sea?*

'Lily!' Then she saw that it was only Jess, running towards her through the wind and rain. 'Lily, are you all right?'

Then Jess's arm was round her and Jess's father was there, wrapping his coat over her shoulders.

'Are you all right?' asked Jess again.

Still shivering, Lily nodded.

'No, you're not!' said Jess. 'You're cold and wet and sad. Your dad said you'd been out for ages!'

As Jess's dad drove them home, Lily pieced together what had happened. Jess and her dad had called to bring them some eggs, and were surprised that Lily was out.

'We knew the weather was getting worse and we tried to phone you, but you must have left yours switched off,' said Jess. 'So we said we'd drive around and look for you.'

The car stopped outside the cottage, where Mum stood in the light of the open door.

'Are you wet through, Lily?' she asked with anxiety in her voice, but she didn't blame Lily or say how worried they'd been – just tucked an arm around her and ushered her indoors.

'Thank you so much, Jess – thank you, Stuart. Lily, you need a hot bath. *Now*. I'll go and run it for you. You get those wet things off, sweetheart.'

'See you tomorrow, Lily,' said Jess, and ran back to the car. There was no need for anything else to be said just now. It could all wait for the morning.

* * *

Jess's diary

I don't know what happened to make Lily run off like that, but I know she's unhappy. Perhaps she'll talk about it later. I hope so.

Malcolm came by for his lesson this morning. It was funny – he stayed afterwards and talked to me about the high school. I said I was OK about it, but he must have known that I wasn't really. He said everyone gets nervous at first, but the island kids look after each other.

He told me the houseparent at the boarding house has a wee Westie dog and it's everyone's friend, and all the boarders spoil it and fuss it and take it for walks. Sometimes, he says, they all go bowling. And he said if anything upsets me I've to tell my teacher, or the houseparent, or him, or anyone, but tell somebody.

I'm glad he said all that. It's as if he read my mind. I feel as if a fog has lifted away.

Dad's just been to the dig site. He says something's up and they're putting tape all round the trench. Perhaps they've found the princess! I knew she was there!

Chapter 8
Where I Belong

Lily stood by her parents and looked at the trench from a distance. It was surrounded by a makeshift fence and some yellow tape with 'biohazard' printed on it.

'Biohazard!' said Lily. She had heard of that. It meant that there were dangerous bacteria about. 'Does that mean it's going to kill us?'

'I hope not,' said Mum, which wasn't encouraging. 'But we phoned the lab about some of the things we found, and ... hi, Jess!'

Jess ran to join them. 'You OK today, Lily?' she asked.

'I'm fine,' said Lily, but she wasn't, and she knew that Jess could tell. 'The site's a biohazard. Mum says it's safe but I'm not going near it.'

'*Nobody's* going near it – that's what the tape is for,' said Mum firmly. 'We've had some test results and this was definitely a hospital site. Some of the medicines they used were very poisonous if they weren't used properly.'

'The diseases weren't too pretty either,' said Dad. 'It's just possible that some of the bacteria have survived in the soil, so we can't go any further with this trench until a specialist team has checked it out.'

'That is disgusting!' said Lily.

'Oh, yes!' said Dad cheerfully. 'There's a drain down there, where they must have got rid of all the—'

'Duncan, be quiet,' said Mum.

'So now,' said Dad, 'we're stuck. Just when we were doing so well! Now we can only get on with Trench Two and we haven't found a trace of anything worth seeing in there yet. Still, we'll get digging.'

'That means that they have to do all the boring stuff first,' Lily whispered to Jess. 'Shall we go to watch the seals? Or go up that hill again? What shall we do?'

'Can we go into Ollerswick?' said Jess. 'I want to get some more pencils and some dog chews for Molly. Tell you what, if we go to the beach first, we can stop at our house for a sandwich and go—'

'To Ollerswick in the afternoon?' suggested Lily.

'And have milkshakes?' said Jess.

* * *

The beach was always a good place for talking. They went down by Selkie's Stair, and when Jess reached the bottom she stopped and put a finger to her lips.

'Look there!' she whispered.

A huge seal sprawled on the rocks, gazing contentedly at nothing. Snuggled beside her was the soft, pale form of her baby. Large dark eyes looked out from its gentle face.

'We won't get close,' whispered Jess as Lily lifted her phone to take a photograph. 'The mothers get distressed if you get too near to their babies.'

They kept their distance from the mother and baby, walking silently to the other end of the bay. But Lily stayed quiet until Jess said, 'What's the matter with you just now?'

They sat down on the sand and Lily, looking at her knees and not at Jess, told her about the conversation last night. When she came to the part about moving to the island there was a little gasp of delight from Jess.

'Wouldn't that be fantastic!' said Jess.

Lily's heart sank. She'd been afraid of this.

'Would it?' she said, still not looking at Jess. 'I mean, in one way it would, because we could see each other all the time and we'd go to school together, unless my parents packed me off somewhere else. But – '

She stopped for a moment to dry her eyes with the heel of her hand.

'It's not my life,' she continued. 'I mean, not permanently. When I first came here I didn't think I'd like it, but I did, and we met and it made all the difference. There's a lot about it that I love. I love this beach and how friendly everybody is. The ceilidh was fantastic! And the freedom! But I just can't imagine living here all the time. I'm used to city things. I'm used to loads of traffic, and big shops and crowds. That's been my life since I was little.'

She raised her head and looked out to sea, not noticing anything. Like the seal, she stared out at nothing. Jess stayed quiet.

That's what I was afraid of, thought Lily. *I've upset Jess because I don't want to stay here.*

'Sorry,' she said. 'Jess, are you all right?'

There was a long pause. Finally, Jess said, 'Oh aye. I was just thinking about what it would be like if it were the other way about, and I had to leave here and go to Edinburgh. I don't even want to go to high school, let alone Edinburgh. It would be too busy for me, just the way the island's too quiet for you. It would be fun for a wee holiday, but I don't think I could get used to it. So I know what you mean.'

Lily found she liked Jess even more for saying that.

'It's all a bit sudden,' she said. 'It just came as a shock – that's why I ran out of the house last night. I don't think Mum and Dad have made their minds up.'

'We'll have to wait and see, then,' said Jess. 'Wouldn't it be easier if we were selkies! We could hang around here, then swim round to the Firth of Forth and see Edinburgh.'

'Can they swim that far?' asked Lily.

'I don't know, but we could always get a lift on a boat!' said Jess, and her laughter made Lily feel a lot more relaxed.

'Mum and Dad are always having big ideas,' she said. 'Staying here is their big idea just now, but they might change their minds. Mum and Dad, and some of their friends, are super-brainy. But super-brainy people can be ... you know – '

'Different?' suggested Jess.

'Clueless!' said Lily, and Jess laughed. 'Very clever, but clueless about ordinary things. Dad keeps all his appointments on his phone, but he forgets to check it and turns up late anyway. My auntie comes twice a year to take Mum shopping or she'd wear the same clothes until they fell apart. They're lovely, and they're my mum and dad, and I'm used to it, but this was such a shock! It's like being a selkie. They can leave the water and live on the land, but they always yearn for the water, and sooner or later they have to go back. I know where I belong. I'm an Edinburgh selkie.'

'If you go back to Edinburgh, you could still come here on holidays,' said Jess hopefully.

'Yes, please!' said Lily. 'And would you come to stay with us in Edinburgh?'

'I'd like that,' said Jess. 'I want to see Christmas!'

They said nothing for a while, watching the seal suckling from its mother, then Lily said that she wanted to get her feet wet, and took off her socks and trainers and stepped into the water. Tiny crabs scuttled round her toes and the wet pebbles gleamed as brightly as the seal's eyes.

Jess appeared beside her and curled her toes into the wet sand.

'Your parents have to keep coming back,' she said. 'They have to find the princess.'

'They're more interested in their old hospital,' said Lily. 'But I hope they find the princess.'

Find the princess, Dad, she thought. *Jess so wants you to find her.*

Unna's story

Whatever is happening?

I tried everything I knew! I cried and screamed and held my breath! Usually when I do that my father gives in because he's afraid I'll make myself ill, but last night it didn't work. He's made up his mind to go back to Norway, and I can't bear to leave. Siv was really worried about me. She even tried to give me one of her sleeping draughts to make me rest, but I closed my mouth tightly and wouldn't have it.

I was soon very tired anyway, and I had a pain. I went to bed quietly.

My father says that any of his men who have married local women can stay here if they want to. Siv tells me stories of Norway, and how beautiful it is. There are flowers everywhere, she says, and mountains so high that they have snow on the tops in midsummer. She said it looks magical. I'm sure she's right, but I so love the island.

And now here I am on the shore again, watching the seals. Siv came too, but it's sunny and she fell asleep. The sweetest baby seal is lying there and I wish I could stroke that warm, soft fur. I mustn't, though. The mother would be angry. She should know that I am Unna Olafsdatter and I protect the seals, but she'd be angry anyway.

A gigantic hound comes romping along the shore. Where did that come from? Who does it belong to? Nobody is with it and it's running straight at the seals!

I have seen what an excited dog can do to a seal, so I run, waving my arms and shouting, 'Get out! Out!' It growls and shows me its teeth, but the mother seal has seen it too. Big and blubbery, she pulls herself up the beach. I pick up a big branch of seaweed and wave it at the dog, shouting for Siv.

The dog turns away with Siv shooing and shouting, but I'm so tired now that I can't stay on my feet. I have to concentrate on little breaths because I can't do big ones.

Siv takes me in her arms. Everything hurts and I can't even speak.

And now all is as gentle as fleece. I have no pain at all. Siv is shouting and screaming for help, but I am more happy and peaceful than I have ever been in my life. Nothing hurts any more.

She lifts me and runs up the hill, back towards my father's hall – but I am here, swimming with the selkies, exactly where I love to be.

Chapter 9
The Seal

Siv's story

Our ships are leaving the island, but Olaf's ship has no giant elk skull on the prow. The skull was always on the prow of his ship when he was at sea, a banner when he went into battle, and over the door of his hall when he was on land. The day after our little Unna died, he took it down and walked out across the island alone. He came back without it and nobody dared to ask questions. Maybe he threw it into the sea.

Nobody knows.

Lily's Diary

Grumpy day. Jess and her mum have gone to the mainland so Jess can get her school shoes and sports kit and things, and they're staying overnight. We've been together every day since we met and now I'm out of practice at being the only one. Still, we're texting each other when I can get a signal.

I'll need to get all my school stuff soon too. Thinking about it made Edinburgh come back to me – all those big shops, and the noise, and the Festival crowds. I think I might find it strange at first when I go home.

EVENING

Oh, mega-grump! Another of those terrible storms has blown up and Jess will have to stay on the mainland for an extra day at least, and it's so unfair! We don't have long now before I have to go home and these days are precious! And Mum and Dad are on edge because they've had to stop work again and they're like children with their favourite toy taken away. Some of the team might go home early.

The Wi-Fi's a bit iffy just now too. I suppose if you live here, you get used to it and learn to be very patient. But I haven't been here long, I'm not used to it and I'm not patient.

Everyone suspects that they won't find anything in that second trench SO WHY ARE THEY STILL BOTHERING WITH IT? All the same, for Jess's sake, I hope they find the young princess.

Why 'young' princess? Why do we think she was young? She could have died aged eighty-six for all anybody knows.

I wrote some more of one of our stories, but it's not the same without Jess. When I go home we're going to take turns writing a few paragraphs and emailing them to each other. We'll always stop at an exciting point, when the heroine's locked in a room or she's at sea in an open boat.

Jess says the seals are all right in a storm. I hope she's right.

MIDNIGHT

I can't sleep, so there's no point in trying. This afternoon Dad decided to go into

Ollerswick and stock up on milk and torch batteries and things in case the weather gets any worse. I went with him and walked as near as I could to the harbour – the waves were already rearing up and hurling themselves against the harbour wall as if they were furious at it for being in their way.

They call the waves 'white horses', and I could see why. I could almost see their manes curling and their hooves beating the air.

Now I'm sitting up in bed writing this and the storm is even worse than it was before. It feels as if it could blow the roof off or the windows in, or just pick up the whole house, carry it away and drop us all in the sea.

The wind shrieks. Whatever strange things people used to believe in, I can understand why. The waves must be massive by now. I hope all the boats in the harbour are safe, and the houses near it. What will the island look like when it's all over?

Will it ever be over?

Lily woke to a morning so calm and bright that for a moment she thought she had dreamed the storm. Then she sat up and saw what looked like a bit of fencing spread in pieces across the grass, and some torn sacking caught in a thorn bush.

Mum was sitting on the living room floor, scraping her hair into a bun while she looked at plans of the dig spread around her.

'Dad's gone to see if there's been any damage done at the site,' she said. 'Did you get any sleep last night?'

'Not much.' She checked the time. She'd slept late – in an hour and a half, the boat would be in. 'Can we phone for the taxi? I want to be at the harbour when the boat comes in.'

The island's only taxi was fully booked for the afternoon. It seemed that everyone wanted to meet the boat. However, Jess's dad phoned and asked if they'd like a lift, and in the meantime Lily walked with Mum up to the dig site.

The news wasn't good. A lot of very muddy archaeologists trudged glumly about and frowned down into the trench as if it had let them down and they were most disappointed in it. Some of them were talking about going home. One of the cabins had blown over.

Lily, looking out to sea, pointed out some very beautiful rainbows, but the archaeologists were still grumpy. Dad reminded them that the peat preserved things well, so anything they did find might be in very good condition, but it didn't seem to make any difference.

'Never mind,' he said cheerfully. 'If some of the team have to leave early, the rest of us can just do more digging!'

That didn't help much either. Lily was about to ask who exactly he meant by 'the rest of us' when she remembered how many of the islanders had joined in to help, and how keen they were. That made her feel better about it.

* * *

At one o'clock Lily was at the harbour jigging from one foot to the other as the boat came near, then Jess was leaning over the rail and waving to her. Lily jumped up and waved back, and soon they were in the cafe drinking milkshakes and talking unstoppably.

'Dad says the waves were right over the harbour wall last night,' said Jess. 'Usually we only get storms this bad in the autumn.'

'Can we get to the shore?' asked Lily. 'See what's been washed up?'

'We'll have to be careful in case there's any damage,' said Jess. 'Jackie's Bay should be all right – it's not so very steep there.'

They fetched Molly, who hadn't had a proper long walk during the storm, and for mile after mile they roamed the island. Here and there they cleared away branches and bits of debris from the road, but there was no sign of any rockfalls. On the Braid, a gentle breeze blew in their faces and the sea was calm, with the tide coming in.

'It looks as if it's saying it didn't do anything last night,' said Lily.

'What is?' asked Jess.

'The sea,' explained Lily. 'It looks so innocent, as if it's saying that it doesn't know anything about last night. It was tucked up in bed with a book and a hot drink.'

'It always does that,' said Jess, then pointed down to something lying on the sand. 'That doesn't look good.'

A seal – a young one still with a little fur – lay on the damp sand of the shore line, not moving. Its eyes were open and a dark patch of blood stained the ground behind it.

'Is it alive?' asked Lily.

They watched. Lily thought she saw its nostrils flare, but she wasn't sure. Then it made an attempt to roll over and flopped back again.

'It might just need to rest and heal, then get back to sea,' said Jess. 'But sometimes they need help and you have to get the wildlife rescue people out.'

'What would they do?' asked Lily.

'Come around by boat and take it to their place on the mainland,' said Jess, and shortened Molly's lead. 'Let's see if we can get a bit closer.'

When they talked about it afterwards, they weren't sure why Molly lunged forward the way she did. Lily caught sight of a rabbit running away and thought that the dog might have been chasing it, or it may have been that Molly noticed the seal, but whichever it was Molly hurled herself forwards, with a furious bark, pulling Jess with her, and they both stumbled. Molly and Jess seemed to sink, but they couldn't be – they were on solid ground …

… but no, no, it wasn't solid ground. As Molly pulled Jess over, the earth gave way beneath them. Lily felt it sink and change – she reached forward to grab Jess's hand, and in that second she remembered that the sensible thing to do would be to spread her weight.

Still hanging on to Jess's hand, she lay down and sprawled on the grass as the ground under her crumbled. She was sliding, Jess's fingers were slipping out of her grasp, and she could no longer see Jess or Molly but she heard a gasp, a shriek, and Molly's frantic barking. Then everything was mud, stones and falling, as she clutched at clumps of grass that gave way in her hand.

She landed on her back, her head spinning. The fall had knocked the breath out of her and she had to snatch air into her lungs in little gasps before she could sit up. When she did, dizziness made her feel sick and the back of her head was hurting.

'Jess?' she said, but her voice sounded thin and weak. She took a deep breath. 'Jess!'

Something pushed against her face. She shied away, then realized that it was only Molly sniffing and licking at her. She scrambled to her feet, wobbled, and had to wait until the whirling in her head had stopped.

'I'm here!' called Jess, but Lily couldn't see her or tell where her voice was coming from.

When she called again, Lily blinked the dust from her eyes and saw a heap of earth and stone that seemed to have Jess's voice inside it.

'Here!' called Jess again, and Lily's eyes focused.

She could see Jess's head and shoulders covered in sand and soil and the way she was struggling to get free from the stones over and around her.

Lily tried to run but it was a lame, painful run before she reached Jess's side and Molly was there before her, nudging at Jess's face and pawing at the stones. Lily caught up, dropping to her knees to scrabble and push at the stones until Jess's hips were free, and then her legs.

Not much blood, just cuts and grazes. Thank goodness for that. Has she broken anything?

'Jess,' she panted, 'does anything hurt?'

Jess nodded with tightly folded lips. 'A bit,' she said. A little at a time she tried to sit up, then lay back again and closed her eyes. Lily removed the last pile of earth from Jess's feet. Blood had soaked into the sand, and there was a deep gash.

'Don't try to move too soon,' said Lily.

'Sorry,' said Jess. 'My head's gone all dizzy.'

'Mine too,' said Lily. 'It's a bit better now, though. What happened?'

'Landslip,' muttered Jess as if she found it hard to think clearly. 'All that rain softening the ground ... and Molly lurching forward like that ... what about you? Have you broken anything?'

'I don't think so, and Molly's all right,' said Lily. Above them, she heard a soft rumbling, then a creak. 'Jess, look out!'

The earth was still moving. Lily wrapped both arms round Jess to heave her up and together they staggered and stumbled to the water's edge.

They had both seen news films on television of derelict buildings being brought down with explosives. The bottom of the building would give way first, then the top would crumble into the empty space. That was exactly what was happening to the shallow cliff above them, and Lily saw that they hadn't moved far enough to be out of the way.

'This way!' she said, and as the cliff gave way they hobbled, stumbled and crawled to the other end of the bay with Molly racing ahead.

Rubble, earth, animal bones and debris of all kinds landed where Jess had just been and they covered their faces against the cloud of dust and dirt, waiting for the noise to stop.

Jess looked up first.

'Is the wee seal all right?' she asked.

Lily stretched up to look. On the other side of the heap of rubble the seal flapped feebly, but only a thin layer of soil had landed on it.

'I think it's OK,' said Lily. 'But you're not,' and the thought of what might have happened – what had nearly happened – made her tremble. 'I can't stop shaking. We could have—'

'Don't think about it,' said Jess sharply, and looked down. 'I lost my shoe on the way down and cut my foot. We need to get out before anything else falls down, and warn everyone that it's dangerous. I blame those rabbits. You know, the rabbits burrowing into the hillside. Did you know your foot's swelling up?'

Lily looked down. There was a puffy bulge above her trainer.

'I hadn't noticed it hurting,' said Lily, but she noticed it now. 'My head hurts too.' She put her hand to the back of her head, but there was no blood. 'I think mostly I'm just bruised. You're a lot worse than I am.'

There were deep grazes down Jess's arms and the gash on her foot looked deep. Dust and mud covered her. 'Am I as dirty as you?' she asked.

'I don't know – how dirty am I?' asked Lily, and suddenly that sounded very funny and they laughed.

'We need to get help for the seal,' insisted Jess, tentatively trying to put her weight on her foot.

'We need to get help for us!' said Lily. 'I don't think either of us can walk very well.'

She reached into her pocket for her phone, but as she took it out she saw that the screen was broken. Then the back dropped off. She tried to push it together, which was difficult as her hands were still shaking, and when she tried to make a call, nothing happened.

'It's broken,' she said.

'I don't know what happened to mine,' said Jess, and nodded towards the heap of rock and rubble. 'I think it's in there somewhere. We'll have to do this by ourselves. We'll have to get up Selkie's Stair.'

Selkie's Stair was steep, but it was the only way up. As Lily said, they had no idea whether it would give way, but they didn't have another choice. Jess tried to walk, and grimaced.

'We can do this together,' she said, determinedly. 'I'll go first.'

Limp, crawl, clamber, scramble, stop for breath, get going again. The top never seemed to get nearer. Sunshine and effort made sweat stand out on Lily's back so that her T-shirt stuck to her uncomfortably. Again they stopped to get their breath back. Molly had run ahead of them.

'If this was one of those stories in books, or in a film,' panted Jess, 'we'd put a message on Molly's collar saying, "Get help!" and she'd run off and find Mum.'

'She'd arrive at the house and paw at the door,' said Lily, 'and they'd say, "Oh! Look! Molly is trying to tell us something! I wonder what it is?"'

'But as it is,' said Jess, with a little gasp of effort as she pulled herself further up the slope, 'she'd just go after a rabbit, lose the note and go home when she got hungry. How are you doing?'

'Nearly there,' said Lily, grasping at one handhold after another. With a last, teeth-gritting effort she hauled herself up on to the cool, damp grass of the Braid.

'Molly, move over. Jess, take my hand. Mind your foot ... '

Exhausted, they sprawled on the grass while seabirds circled and squawked above them.

'Should we shout for help?' suggested Lily.

'Yes, and keep walking until we find somebody,' said Jess. 'Or crawl, or something.'

'OK,' said Lily, and realized that this was one of the great things about her relationship with Jess – that anything, even a time like this, could be an opportunity for a challenge, for teamwork. She lifted her sore foot carefully and tried to hop.

'Race you!' she called.

'You're on!' said Jess.

Chapter 10
Unna and the Elk Skull

Lily's Diary

When we were near the road, Jess got hold of Molly's lead, then Molly saw a rabbit and had a barking fit, so we thought somebody would hear her – but there's nothing unusual about a dog barking, so nothing happened and we were back on our hands and knees when we got to the road.

Crawling across it didn't seem like a good idea, so we kneeled down by the side of it to wave at the first car that came along – and it was the four-wheel drive with Jess's mum driving!

She looked horrified – I'd forgotten what a mess we were. I wanted to calm her down so I kept saying, 'It's all right, it's all right,' and then Jess said that it wasn't all right, so we explained about the landslip and the seal.

After that, the whole island was on it. Men came to put warning signs around the landslip and the wildlife rescue people came by boat for the seal. They phoned to say that she'd been gashed on a rock, or maybe attacked by something, and they'd keep her until she was well and then release her. I'm so glad we saved her.

We thought Jess might need a stitch in her foot, but at the surgery they put those little strips on it so she didn't have to go to the mainland.

Mum put a packet of frozen peas over my ankle. It didn't feel very nice when they melted. We're covered in bruises but neither of us has broken anything at least. I'm writing this now with my foot resting on a chair.

Molly came off all right. She just wants to chase rabbits again!

On the subject of rabbits, Jess was right. The locals all reckon that the warrens had weakened the hillside, and so one more storm was enough to make it unstable.

Apparently, Mum and Dad found something interesting in that second trench – the one that everybody else gave up on – but they haven't said much about it.

> I keep reliving what happened, over and over again. I remember the feeling of falling and not being able to stop it. I don't want to think about what might have happened. Mum's going to sleep in the spare bed in my room tonight.
>
> Oh yes – we're not going to move! Mum said this evening that they're having second thoughts. They still love it here, but it's too remote and they don't want to live in a place where I wouldn't be happy. They still want to keep coming here. (Yes!) They want to hire the cottage again. (Yes!) This will be our second home. (YESSS!)

It was a few days later when Jess and Lily, still limping a little, stood at the side of the Unfell trench. There had been more digging, until it looked as if a slice had been bitten out of the hillside. Lily watched her parents' faces. They had that bright-eyed look, like excited children, when something important was happening.

'Come over here, so you can see properly,' said Mum. 'We've found a kist!'

'What's a kist?' asked Jess.

'A burial chamber,' Lily told her. Then Dad shone the torch, and she gasped.

There it was. It was real. It was true.

A small skeleton lay on the ground, the bones so fine that it seemed impossible that they hadn't crumbled. The body had been laid curled up on its side, as if asleep. A comb and a cup lay beside it, and something dark on the remains of a crumbled necklace.

'A little girl,' said Mum gently. 'Buried with her comb and a cup, and a necklace.'

Jess turned away.

'Jess, are you all right?' asked Lily, suddenly concerned. She herself was used to seeing ancient graves and skeletons, but Jess wasn't.

Jess quickly wiped tears from her eyes.

'It was a shock,' she said. 'Could she be – ?'

'The Viking princess? I'm pretty certain she is, yes,' said Dad.

'I always knew there was a Viking princess,' said Jess, as Lily slipped an arm round her. 'But she was always a story – and now she's real. And she was so little!'

Dad picked up the dark pebble. He rubbed it with a cloth and held it up to the light.

'What a lovely thing!' he said. 'It's still very dirty, but it's amber, set in silver! It must have been very precious to her. Only a girl from a wealthy family would have something like this.'

Mum and Dad took photographs and measurements.

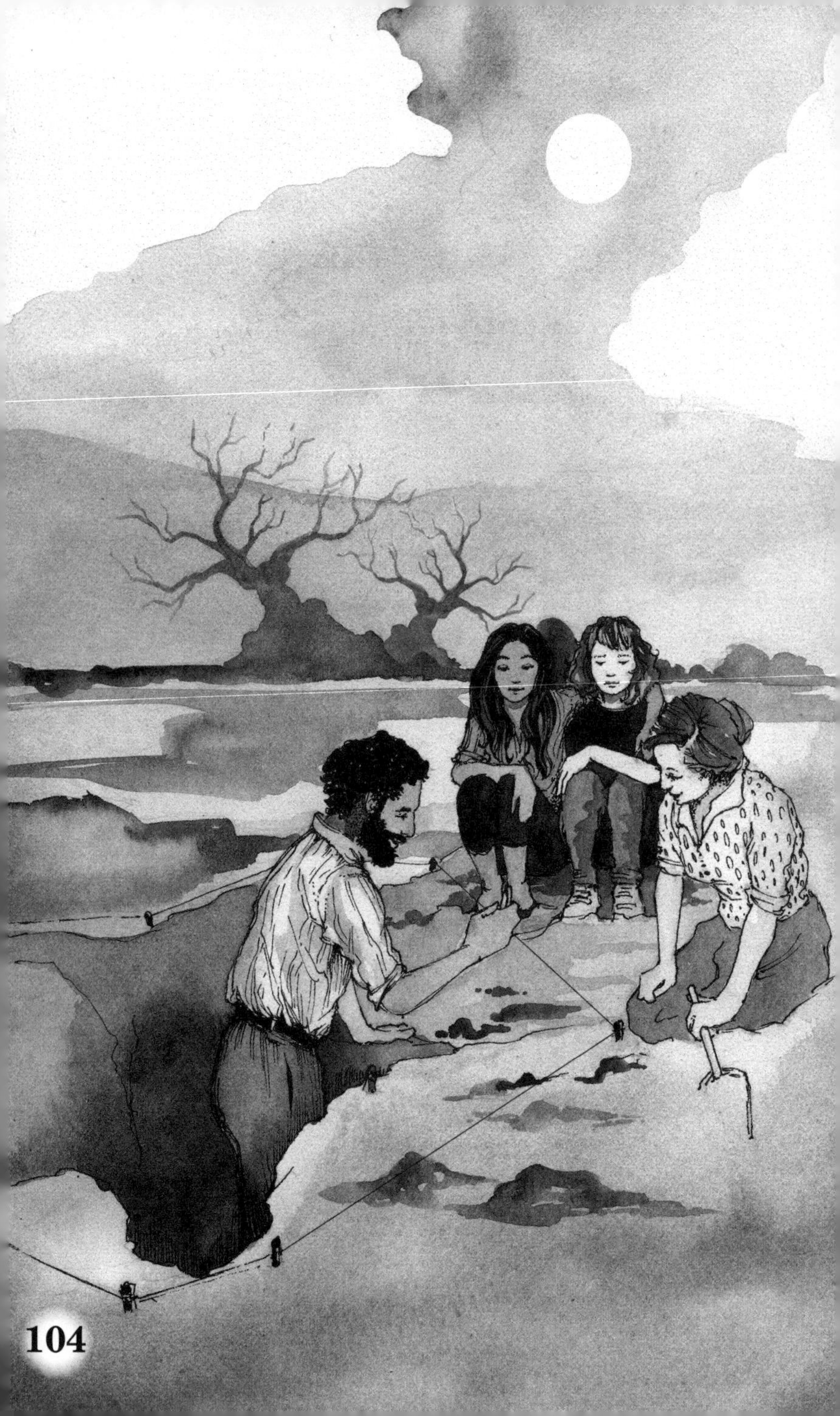

They began covering the site with tarpaulins and making phone calls. Before the trench was completely covered Jess kneeled down and whispered something into the grave, and Lily didn't ask what it was.

* * *

The evening was cold and they lit the fire in the cottage. Lily gazed into it, listening to the crack and mutter of the wood as it burned. The news that the princess's grave had been found had reached Ollerswick and the whole island was talking about it. Somebody from the local paper had phoned for an interview.

She thought of the princess. *Now we've found you,* she thought. *Now we've proved you existed. A girl – not a legend, not a seal. But we don't know a thing about you.*

'Will we ever know her name, or anything about her?' she asked.

'It's unlikely,' said Mum. 'The grave proves that there were Vikings here, but no more than that. She must have been a nobleman's daughter, but we don't know whose.'

'Olaf Elkskull?' suggested Lily.

'We still can't prove that he was here,' said Mum. 'There are no records of him having a daughter, but that's not surprising if she died when she was a child. The wee girl in the grave didn't have her own story.'

'Yes, she did,' said Lily. 'But nobody ever told it.'

105

***

There were two more days of photography, sketching and writing up notes before Lily and her family had to go home.

Lily and Jess made the most of every second. They wrote stories, drew pictures, watched seals and ran along beaches with Molly. They'd sit on the harbour wall, or drink milkshakes at the cafe. Sometimes, they helped with the work of clearing up the debris following the storm.

On Lily's last evening on the island, when all the cases were packed and there seemed nothing much to do, there was a knock at the cottage door.

Dad went to answer it and found Malcolm on the doorstep, carrying a sack.

'I hope it's not a bad time to call, Professor Walker,' he said. 'Only some of us found this at the bay when we were clearing up the rubble after the landslip, the one where Jess and your Lily fell down. It's not the sort of thing we've ever found on the island before. We didn't know if we should move it but it could have been washed out to sea with the next tide, so we fetched it away. At first we thought it was from a deer, but it isn't. Do you know what it is?'

From the bag he drew out something white and bony. It was clearly some sort of animal skull, but very big, and looked incomplete as if parts of it had broken off. Here and there, tarnished metal clung to it.

Dad took it in his hands and fell silent.

'I know exactly what that is,' he said at last. He seemed calm, but Lily knew that tone of voice. There was a keen edge to it.

His hands shook a little as he turned the skull round and held it to the light.

'Well, well,' he said. 'It's an elk skull, but I've never seen one this big. I think we really are rewriting history. If I'm right about this, Malcolm, this was the skull of a giant of an elk that roamed Norway over a thousand years ago. It's been covered in silver. This is all the evidence we need. It came here by sea on the prow of a longship and was nailed up over the door of Olaf Elfskull's hall.'

And that little girl saw it every day, thought Lily, and it was as if the elk skull and the little princess were alive to her – as if she had a brief glimpse through a window and saw the young princess laughing, playing, holding up her necklace to the light to make it sparkle. She put her hand round the white bone and understood, not for the first time, why her parents so loved their work.

Lily's Diary

Jess and I cried this morning. And laughed. And made charts of how long it will be before half-term. When she wasn't looking, I bought a card. I'll post it to her school so it's there to meet her. (I drew a selkie on it.) I left it until the very last minute to walk up the gangway, and Jess waved until the boat was out of sight.

As the engine thrummed and the deck began to sway under Lily's feet, she turned to face the island and wave to Jess. The family had already arranged their next visit to the island and Jess's first trip to stay with them in Edinburgh.

When the island was only a green jewel in the turquoise sea, she turned to face the mainland, looking for Jess's school and thinking of her own, and who her teachers would be, and whether she could join a drama club. Already, she was looking forward to being home. Already, she was looking forward to coming back.

She took out her notebook and began to write.

Afterword

Scottish dialect

Scottish people have some different words which are not used elsewhere. Here are the ones used in this book:

aye: yes

blowing a hooly: extremely windy

fash yourself: feel worried or upset

in a stooshie: making a fuss, in a state

just now: at the moment

messages: errands

neeps and haggis: traditional Scottish dish. 'Neeps' means mashed swede, and a 'haggis' is minced offal, onions, spices and oatmeal all cooked in a sheep's stomach.

wee: small

will I ... ? : shall I ... ?

Scottish Gaelic

As well as speaking a Scottish dialect, in which some words are different to English, some Scottish people speak a completely different language called Gaelic or Scottish Gaelic.

Scottish festivals

This book mentions some of the events and festivals which are important in Scotland.

Burns Night
Date: 25th January

This is a celebration of Robert Burns, Scotland's national poet. People gather for a 'Burns Supper' where they eat Scottish dishes like neeps and haggis and recite Burns's poetry.

Edinburgh Festival
Date: Three weeks in August

This is the biggest arts festival in the world. It takes place all over Edinburgh.

Hogmanay
Date: New Year's Eve

In Scotland, people have a huge party called Hogmanay on New Year's Eve which carries on into New Year's Day.

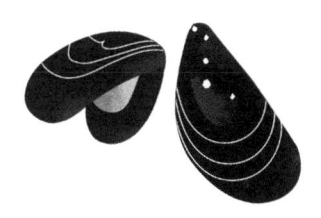

A note on Unna's condition
In the story, Unna has a heart condition which can easily be treated now, but was very dangerous in Viking times.

About *Warrior Scarlet*
Warrior Scarlet was written by Rosemary Sutcliff and published in 1958. It's set during the Bronze Age and is about a boy who wants to become a warrior.